VACANT A DIARY OF THE PUNK YEARS 1976–79

VACANT A DIARY OF THE PUNK YEARS 1976–79

Nils Stevenson
photographs by Ray Stevenson

With 158 photographs, 21 in colour

Thames and Hudson

Dedicated to the fabulous failures who made this thing happen, particularly Stiv Bators, Tracey O'Keefe, Jerry Nolan, Johnny Thunders, Nancy Spungen and Sid Vicious, RIP.
Many thanks to everyone who took the time to rake over the coals and contribute texts:

Gaye Advert – local government officer

Viv Albertine – film maker

Simon Barker – art dealer

Andy Blade – aspiring rock-group manager

Rob Collins – record company executive

Gail Higgins – retailer

Alan Jones – film critic and author

Jordan – veterinary nurse and breeder of champion Burmese cats

Don Letts – video and film maker

Walter Lure – stockbroker/musician

Fachtna O'Ceallaigh – music business consultant/manager

Mark P – writer/musician

Marco Pirroni – guitarist and record producer

Roadent – gobo artist

Steve Severin – writer/musician

Paul Simonon – painter/musician

Simone – dominatrix

T.V. Smith – musician

Helen Wellington-Lloyd – wise performer

Special thanks to Dan Marks and Marco Pirroni for their help and patience.

PAGE 1: SEX PISTOLS IN TELEPHONE BOX
PAGE 2: BOO, NILS'S ASSISTANT, IN SIOUXSIE AND THE BANSHEES' OFFICE
PAGE 4: SID VICIOUS DOLL
PAGE 5: SEX PISTOLS HANDOUT

British Library Cataloguing-in-Publication Data
A catalogue record for this book is available from the British Library

ISBN 0-500-28103-3

Printed in Hong Kong by H & Y Printing Limited

CONTENTS

WORLD'S END: PUNK'S BEGINNINGS

Only criminals and artists defy rules – Diderot

In 1974 a shocking-pink padded sign announcing SEX was erected above a shop at World's End. Scrawled on the wall beneath was Rousseau's dictum: 'Craft Must Have Clothes But Truth Loves To Go Naked.'

Inside, leather jackets and trousers hung on gymnasium parallel bars. Rubber masks, handcuffs and harnesses, ripped T-shirts and fluffy mohair sweaters were among the sensory delights on offer. A jukebox, stocked with early rock 'n' roll, added nostalgic pop references. The walls were covered in foam and sprayed with phrases from the pornographic novels of Alexander Trocchi and excerpts from Valerie Solanas's manifesto for SCUM (The Society For Cutting Up Men) in pink and red paint.

Malcolm McLaren and Vivienne Westwood's shop at the wrong end of the King's Road adulterated conventional youth styles, mixing radical political rhetoric with the fetish wear of the middle-aged and middle-class. SEX was a Bizarro world in which norms were reversed in what the proprietors considered the true spirit of rock 'n' roll. It asserted the value of the worthless, revelled in the perverse and celebrated criminal behaviour, and it quickly became a meeting point for petty criminals, prostitutes, perverts and freaks.

For nearly a decade the King's Road had been lined with the Ferraris, Corvettes and Bentleys of the 'New Aristocracy' – '60s pop stars, famous photographers and young advertising executives – who met at the Roebuck pub on the corner of Beaufort Street and the King's Road. In 1974, this was where the motley SEX crew rubbed shoulders with the Led Zeppelin entourage (whose offices were at World's End), Marc Bolan and Gary Glitter (who shopped at Alkasura near Beaufort Street), the owners of Granny Takes A Trip (who supplied the Faces and the Rolling Stones), and assorted rock-star wives and groupies whom Paul Cook describes as, 'Old birds who'd split from rock-star husbands.'

The harsh style of the few (and there were very few in 1974) aficionados of SEX, dressed in every shade of black, were in startling contrast to the dandified fashions of the New Aristocracy in their colourful velvet suits and

satin loons. Although the SEX crew were tolerated by these members of the nouveau-riche Chelsea set, they were regarded as freaks.

At that time I had a stall in Beaufort Market near the Roebuck. In an attempt to cash in on any one of the many revivals of the time, I was selling a pot-pourri of '50s drapes, '60s fleck-and-leather jackets, American T-shirts, winklepickers, plastic sandals and drainpipe trousers. I knew the Roebuck crowd because the pub was my local, but, although I worked only a few doors away from Malcolm and Vivienne and often saw them in the pub, I did not meet either of them until I moved in with June Child (one of those 'old birds' who had split from her rock-star husband Marc Bolan). Having worked for Blackhill Enterprises, who represented Pink Floyd among others, June Child was well schooled in the music business and was, in some part, responsible for Bolan's success. When Malcolm was in the pub he would invariably interrogate June about the biz and tell us about a group of teenagers he was managing who, he reckoned, were going to be the next Bay City Rollers. He also ranted about art, the passion that first connected us.

DEMANDING THE IMPOSSIBLE

Between the early 1960s and early 1970s the numbers of students attending art schools rose by seventy per cent, and, like many working-class kids, that's where Malcolm and I found an education. In 1969 I went to Barnet Art College which had one of the first Environmental Design courses in the country, regarded by a small but enthusiastic clique as at the cutting edge of art education. The aim of the course was to explore the environment using a combination of fine art and conceptual practices. Trees were decorated with paper, car parks cordoned off with string and cars painted with generic pop symbols like the American flag. We saw all this as the means to liberate art from the narrow confines of the conventional gallery space and from the similarly narrow world of British

OPPOSITE: SEX BUSINESS CARD

establishment figures who ran them. Although several galleries, such as the Lisson and Signals, were established in the 'counterculture' to show the new radical works, the idea of a gallery of any sort – with its implications of cultural authority and contextual appropriateness – was anathema to me. To make the point that art should not be evaluated like any other commodity or cheapened by rank commercialism, I started to set fire to my work as soon as it was completed so that it was impossible for my tutors to assess it. By this time, the concept of art had become so difficult for me that neither I nor any of my contemporaries at art school could even say the word without an ironic twist and an embarrassed smile. Defining what it was became a major preoccupation for the next five years. It was around that time that I became aware of the work of Walter Benjamin whose seminal text *The Work Of Art In The Age Of Mechanical Reproduction* (1935) had, I felt, identified the principal problematic of twentieth-century art: 'An analysis of art in the age of mechanical reproduction must do justice to these relationships, for they lead us to an all-important insight: for the first time in world history, mechanical reproduction emancipates the work of art from its parasitical dependence on ritual. To an ever greater degree the work of art becomes the work of art designed for reproducibility. From a photographic negative for example, one can make any number of prints; to ask for the "authentic" print makes no sense. But when the instant criterion of authenticity ceases to be applicable to artistic production, the total function of art is reversed. Instead of being based on ritual, it begins to be based on another practice – politics.' At the time that I became acquainted with Benjamin's theories I also became interested in Andy Warhol who, apart from then being the art world's prime mover, seemed to me to have instinctively understood the points Benjamin was making, and to be almost uniquely capable of expressing them in his art. His prints were impersonal reproductions, corporate in tone, which seemed to laud the consumer society to which they referred. Yet it was the same consumer-led culture that created the damaged individuals who inhabited the Factory. And this was the same society that spawned the primitive sound of the Factory's in-house group, the Velvet

Underground, who were the most uncommercial and exciting group I had ever heard. What I particularly admired in the work coming out of the Factory was that these contradictions were left unresolved – they were allowed to be contradictory – which seemed appropriate, and certainly expressed my general mood of ambivalence.

Despite my difficulty in defining what it was, I regarded being an artist as the noblest of all pursuits, an attitude which led to my expulsion from art school in 1971 when I made what I felt was the ultimate artistic statement by stopping painting altogether. Much more to my taste was the art I had done from 1967 to 1968, which consisted of flying kites on Parliament Hill with Yoko Ono and prancing about with the concept artist David Medalla's avant-garde dance troupe Exploding Galaxy. I discovered the pleasures of the senses 'where every heart was generous and all wines flowed', as Rimbaud wrote. And I also discovered that far from being incompatible with art practice, I could assert that the pursuit of the sensual was the art practice. It was a discovery that would deeply affect the direction that my life would take.

While I was maintaining romantic purity in Barnet, Malcolm McLaren, who was then using his stepfather's surname Edwards, was living with his grandmother in South Clapham and attending Goldsmiths Art College. During his time at Goldsmiths, he became involved with an agit-prop group called King Mob – England's answer to the Situationists whose philosophy was dominating French intellectual life and the radical Parisian politics of the time. Dick Pountain describes his first encounter with Malcolm and King Mob at the LSE sit-in: 'The New Left people were telling them to be serious and responsible, and King Mob telling them to get their rocks off, let it all hang out, etc. It was very iffy, because the great mass in the middle were swaying both ways. Only a minority supported us; the majority wanted to be quiet and respectable, but these two guys came out of the crowd and joined with us and said, "We're with you." They were a couple of art students from Goldsmiths and one was called Fred Vermorel and the other was Malcolm Edwards. They both had long, dirty khaki macs, a couple of impoverished art students. And of course Malcolm went on to finer things and became Malcolm

McLaren, and in a lot of ways the whole Sex Pistols scam was the putting into practice of a lot of Situationist theories.' (J. Green, *Days in the Life*, 1988.)

The Situationist International (SI) was a quasi-anarchistic group formed in Paris in 1957, a political evolution from the avant-garde ideas of Dada and Surrealism earlier in the century. The aim of their political philosophy was to re-empower the proletariat, whose lives were summed up in the Situationist slogan: *metro – boulot – TV – dodo* (subway – work – TV – sleep). They felt that in what they dubbed the Society of the Spectacle people had turned into consumers of mediated events, mediated ideas and mediated actions, and that their role was to challenge that enforced passivity by breaking down the barriers between direct and mediated experience. The artist depicting situations and feelings was merely colluding with the forces that created the Society of the Spectacle. The role of the artist, as they saw it, was to create challenging situations.

To those ends, the Situationists, chief among them Guy Debord, waged a campaign which included publishing pamphlets and daubing provocative graffiti on monuments and walls around Paris. But it was during *les evénements* of May '68 that the Situationist project really took off. Ironically, the spectacle of police attacking student demonstrators was irresistible to the media (of which Debord was so critical). The TV and newspaper reports fuelled discontent in the country, and led to a general strike.

The Situationists' attempt to break down the barriers between art and life encouraged demonstrations and terrorism by validating them as artistic acts. In this sense, they filled the gap between the vogue for conceptual gestures and the commercial plastic arts which they saw as part of the despised Society of the Spectacle. It was these impulses and intellectual currents that were so attractive to the young Malcolm Edwards at art school, and he found himself intellectually and emotionally drawn towards the English offshoot of the Situationists, King Mob.

The founders of King Mob began their political activism around 1965 as the English branch of the SI. In July 1966 they published the first edition of the magazine *Heatwave* which contained material from

American anarchist publications such as *Rebel Worker*. However, there were soon disagreements with Debord. The English group were in favour of youth culture and particularly keen on delinquents like the Teddy Boys and the Ton-up Kids (the bikers who aimed to reach and exceed 100 mph, 'the ton'). They were also condemned by the French for their incorrect attitude towards certain elements of American counterculture which reinforced the Society of the Spectacle. In late 1967 Debord expelled the English branch from Situationist International. Christopher Gray and the Wise brothers promptly formed King Mob.

The group's name came from the Gordon Rioters of 1780 who scrawled 'His Majesty King Mob' on the walls of Newgate prison, and rampaged through London, opening prisons and releasing their inmates. The group's aim, according to Dave Wise, was to 'laud and practise active nihilism....Instead of openly political causes, King Mob celebrate any delinquent or anti-social activity.' Their techniques included crude 'direct action', such as attacking symbols of modern consumerism (like Wimpy Bars), as well as romantic gestures, such as scrawling witty or perverse graffiti on billboard posters – 'I can't breathe', for instance, or lines from Coleridge's 'Dejection: an Ode':
'A grief without a pang, void, dark and drear,
A stifled, drowsy, unimpassioned grief...'

King Mob's most publicised 'situation' took place in 1968 when a group of twenty-five, one dressed as Santa Claus, went to Selfridges and gave away the toys. Malcolm was one of them. They also produced flyers praising Valerie Solanas's shooting of Andy Warhol, and lauded terrorist groups like the Red Army Faction and the Angry Brigade. They compiled a hit-list of artists and pop icons such as Richard Hamilton, David Hockney, Yoko Ono, Mary Quant and Twiggy, and managed to produce a few issues of a newspaper called *The King Mob Echo*, which praised (among others) Jack the Ripper and the child murderer Mary Bell. And Christopher Gray came up with the idea of creating a shite pop group, hyping the shit out of them and then exposing them as crap.

Insofar as they were all attempting to break down the barriers between art and life, there were similarities between what King Mob, David Medalla's Exploding Galaxy and the Environmental Design course at Barnet Art College were doing. But King Mob ideology favoured 'direct action' over obstructing car-parks, kite-flying or arty prancing in the street, and, in his final years as a student at Goldsmiths, Malcolm started smashing the windows of Wimpy Bars.

Christopher Gray said that Malcolm was 'just another wide-eyed art student – he wasn't very involved.' Nevertheless, many of the achievements and ideas of King Mob were to recur as Malcolm's own in ways that echoed Karl Marx's dictum that 'events and personages occur twice, the first time as tragedy, the second as farce.' Bernard Rhodes, who at the time was hawking clothes up and down the King's Road and who, much later would manage the Clash, produced a version of the King Mob hit list on a T-shirt for Malcolm and Vivienne. Their 'Cambridge Rapist' T-shirt was in the spirit of King Mob's praise for Mary Bell, while extracts from Valerie Solanas's SCUM manifesto were spray-painted on the walls of SEX. The support for the Teddy Boys and Ton-up Kids found its expression in Malcolm and Vivienne Westwood's forays into fashion in their first shops, Let It Rock, and Too Fast to Live, Too Young To Die. But perhaps the most striking connection between Malcolm and King Mob was the similarity between the rhetoric that Malcolm would later use to describe the Sex Pistols and the template for subverting the record industry that Christopher Gray had developed.

'LET IT ROCK' KNICKERS

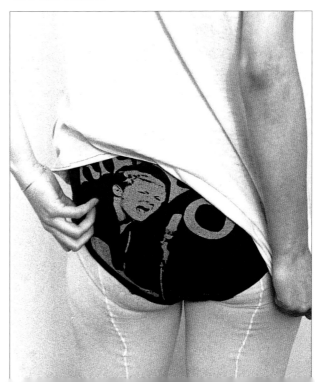

Gray's proto-punk impulse was tragic in the sense that while he articulated it and understood its power, he didn't or couldn't do it. And Malcolm's later attempt to carry it out was farcical because he never noticed that the Sex Pistols could play and were, in fact, rather good.

A NATION OF SHOPKEEPERS

In May 1971, the Angry Brigade bombed Biba's superstore on Kensington High Street – the most fashionable shop in London. In so doing they achieved what had seemed impossible, 'alienating the political and fashion wings of the underground from each other' (Tom Vague, *Anarchy in the UK: The Angry Brigade*, 1997). But that event did not diminish Malcolm's belief in the power of clothing and the artistic potential of the boutique which had developed in tandem with pop music.

In the catalogue for the 1998 New York exhibition 'Impresario: Malcolm McLaren, The British New Wave', Jane Withers wrote: 'The boutique played a cathartic role by providing a stage for pop culture's characteristic synthesis of the mutually sustaining iconographies of Pop Art, pop music and pop fashion. For an emergent generation of artistic activators, the boutique environment presented a vehicle for effecting the artists' transfer, as McLuhan observed, from "the ivory tower to the control tower of society". The pop boutique as it evolved in the '60s offered the possibility of an environment that was both artistic and a commercial outlet – a fusion of studio and gallery, court and stage. ... [As Malcolm McLaren says,] "The shop was a replacement for being an artist in another way. You didn't want to paint pictures in the 1970s. You'd come out of the whole environmental school of thinking, that whole conceptual art." '

The handful of shops in the World's End that had become the most influential arbiters of fashion, style and taste were follies with extravagant frontages and interiors. Nigel Weymouth and John Pearce, for instance, cut a car in two and created the illusion that it was driving out of Granny Takes a Trip, while John Lloyd, a lovable eccentric, notorious for cruising the King's Road in a monk's habit,

fingering rosary beads, turned his shop Alkasura into an Aladdin's cave of glitz and gloss complete with fountain.

As well as these environmental developments in the retail sector, there had been a number of fashion revivals since the late '60s, and in the early '70s London was awash with the iconography from the recent past and imaginary future. The flood of revivals was driven in part by Hollywood films which romanticised various eras and icons such as '20s gangsters (*Bonnie and Clyde*, 1967), rebel hippie bikers (*Easy Rider*, 1969) or '50s America and James Dean (*The Last Picture Show*, 1971). The past was a treasure trove of ideas to be plundered, and secondhand clothing provided the means for many people to start their own little shops and then develop their own quirky ideas. Tommy Roberts had moved from secondhand military wear to making T-shirts with appliqué stars and sequins, which he sold to Elton John and others at Mr Freedom on Kensington Church Street (the shop was stuffed with eight-foot-high blue gorillas and giant television counters). Barbara Hulanicki's Biba was decorated in the Art Deco style and reproduced the glamorous artefacts of the '30s for mass consumption.

It was in this context that Malcolm discovered 430 King's Road. At that time the shop was called Paradise Garage and had a '50s ambience with a jukebox blaring away in a completely black interior. Impressed by the blue Lurex trousers that Vivienne had made for Malcolm, Bradley Mendelson, who managed the shop, approached him and proposed a deal. Malcolm, his friend Patrick Casey and Vivienne moved into the back of Paradise Garage where they started selling secondhand records. Soon after this, Mendelson's boss Trevor Miles arrived back from honeymoon, declared himself bankrupt and walked away, leaving Malcolm, Casey and Vivienne with the whole shop. Casey disappeared to Spain. And then there were two.

Surprisingly, given Malcolm's ideological roots, he and Vivienne did much the same with Paradise Garage as Barbara Hulanicki had done at the Biba superstore, only with a different era. While Hulanicki recreated the 1930s in Kensington High Street, Malcolm and Vivienne renamed the shop Let it Rock, and turned 430 King's Road into an oasis of 1950s camp nostalgia, decorating it with original

'50s wallpaper and posters, '50s cabinets and magazines, jars of Brylcreem and guitar-shaped mirrors. Although others were selling '50s clothing and memorabilia, Malcolm and Vivienne's concern for authenticity bordered on the fanatical, and they sold only pristine drape jackets, drainpipe trousers and other Ted garb, all beautifully pressed and folded. The shop quickly attracted the hard-core Teddy Boy clientele whom King Mob had held in such high esteem.

The '70s Teds were not so much a part of a revival as a resurgence. The style was well established, almost reassuring, having survived almost intact since the '50s. Ted style had a historical context which made its meanings overt. The messages in the first English rock 'n' roll style were clear: British, working-class and heterosexual.

THE GREATEST SHOW ON EARTH

Ever since I first saw a Teddy Boy from my pram in the East End of London, I had been drawn to youth culture. But I knew nothing about the Teds' stylistic origins until I left college in 1971 and went to work for Richard Buckle, ballet critic of the *Sunday Times*. As a cockney (born within the sound of Bow bells and living in the East End until I was twelve), I loathed the British class system, and, as part of the new avant-garde, I wanted to drag art out of the gallery. Yet soon after I first met Richard Buckle at Andy Warhol's first major British exhibition at the Tate Gallery, I found myself working with this pillar of the establishment to raise money to buy Titian's *Death of Actaeon* for the nation, and involved in Dicky's other pet project, setting up the Theatre Museum in Covent Garden (which, coincidentally, now houses all the Sex Pistols' art works).

My role required me to wear a purple mock-Edwardian suit (designed by Dicky), pour drinks for celebrities at junkets, and mince around Covent Garden in silver shoes. For the gala benefit, *The Greatest Show on Earth* held at the Coliseum on 22 June 1971, Dicky's prized possession, Picasso's curtain for *Le Train Bleu*, was taken out of storage for service on the stage. The performers included Rudolph Nureyev, Margot Fonteyn, Zizi Jeanmaire, Karma

TEDS ROCKING, 1970S

Dev, Wayne Sleep and a host of other celebrated dancers, as well as some of the artists on King Mob's hit list. More funds were raised by a sale of versions of the Titian by David Hockney, Duncan Grant and Jean Hugo. The evening was a great success.

Dicky Buckle was an ex-Scots guard and aesthete who loved rough trade. In the 1940s he and his cohorts had created an extraordinary world of upper-class foppishness in an attempt to return to the values of the Edwardian era – a golden age for the aristocracy. They idealised its fashions, donning long, tight-waisted jackets, tight trousers and flamboyant waistcoats. Some favoured black velvet collars, which originally signified mourning for the death of the French aristocracy in the French Revolution. Ironically this look was bastardised by some working-class kids who reflected a grotesque mirror-image back to the establishment. The tabloids of the '50s abbreviated the pompous name New Edwardian, and the Teddy Boy was born. Within this culture were the seeds of all that followed, and clothes became a means of escape for the underclass.

But by the 1970s things had changed. This was a society where the so-called New Aristocracy showed the way for anyone who wished to express themselves, and defined the aspirations of the emergent teenager. There was considerably greater class mobility, which weakened the symbolic acts of resistance of Teddy-boy style.

This was at a time when David Bowie had completed his transition from folk singer/mime to androgynous rock-god – he had 'come out' at the beginning of the decade, and was encouraging his adolescent audience to experiment with their sexuality. Camp was in, and Roxy Music's sterile pop-scapes were popular. Ignoring the economic crisis, the acolytes of Bowie and Roxy Music revelled in the

DAVID BOWIE

joy of the inauthentic. With an eye to an androgynous, sci-fi world in which society's constraints vanished on a Martian disco floor, the total sham became de rigueur.

Teds were anachronistic in this landscape. With the exception of Dickie Buckle and his highly camp entourage, the upper-class New Edwardian look was no more, and the style which had been its mirror image was now adrift and freakish-looking. Unlike the originators of the style, the new Teds did not question the established order, they accepted it by attempting to live in a permanent past. In the '50s, Teds' dress announced they did not know their place. In the '70s, it said they did.

This, the first British, working-class, rock 'n' roll, youth cult provided the foundation for much of what was to follow – even in the sense that it had its origins in queer culture. But the purism with which Let it Rock pursued the goal of authenticity was regressive in the sense that it neither recognised nor embraced the Ted's complex and transgressive roots.

BACK TO THE FUTURE

Malcolm and Vivienne were searching for the means to shock the bourgeois sensibility and, sticking with the spirit of King Mob, Let it Rock picked up on the style of another dated bunch of delinquents, the Hispanic Pachucos from the '40s, developing a version of their Zoot Suit.

For Malcolm and Vivienne, as for most of the shops in the King's Road, the Glam phenomenon of 1972 was a turning point. Paul Cook says, 'Glam forced Malc and Viv to change. It was great seeing the Teds' faces when they changed. It was like, "What the fuck's going on here?" That dreaded word change, they couldn't handle it.' Contrary as ever, they started getting interested in the style of the Ton-up Kids, and changed the name of the shop from Let it Rock to Too Fast to Live, Too Young to Die. Rockers had the distinct advantage over Teds and Pachucos of appearing dirty: dirt signifying the ultimate terror of the middle class – chaos.

The changes at 430 King's Road were accelerated after Malcolm went to a screening of Kenneth Anger's film *Scorpio Rising* at the Arts Lab. The film's combination of homoerotica, magic and the American-biker look were to provide a stock of images and shocking juxtapositions that were perhaps as influential in the development of punk style as were the thoughts and writings of King Mob. Film critic Sheldon Renan's description of *Scorpio Rising* identifies much of its fundamental iconography as well as its techniques: 'Anger saw pop songs, drug use, motorcycle cultists, the teenage fad of Nazi symbols, and so on, as strong manifestations of fomenting demonic forces. The "hero", Scorpio, is intercut with shots of Hitler, James Dean, Marlon Brando, and Jesus Christ shown in scenes from a religious movie. A rough homosexual party of the cyclists is blended with footage of Christ meeting his disciples, a cycle race with Jesus on the donkey entering Jerusalem.' (*The Underground Film*, 1967.)

Malcolm and Vivienne moved in on the queer as delinquent, and, in the tradition of the bricoleur, they created a bizarre assortment of clothes from the materials that were readily at hand: chicken bones from a local restaurant spelt out 'PERV' and 'ROCK' on black, capped-sleeved T-shirts, and on others chrome studs (left behind in the shop by Trevor Miles) proclaimed 'Venus'. They ripped soft-porn photos out of their '50s magazines and installed them under gelatin on T-shirts, and they stole prints from the gay artist Tom of Finland's books of nude cowboys and other gay 'clones'. Malcolm's and Vivienne's response to *Scorpio Rising* seemed sound both commercially and artist-ically. There was, after all, an audience for a new, harder gay look, and in the early '70s sexual politics were in.

Although all the iconography was familiar, the new contexts and novel juxtapositions were fresh. Nothing like them had been seen before, yet they appeared old, battered. Indeed the references to Chuck Berry and Little Richard left over from Let It Rock T-shirts were antiquated. But instead of trying to make them look modern, Malcolm and Vivienne distressed the fabrics, ripped them and dyed them oily colours. The clothes were impossible to place in history: it was as if they were from some distant place or parallel universe beyond the conventions of rock 'n' roll mythology.

Malcolm and Vivienne's 'painterly' new artefacts with their fetishes and banal symbols managed to capture the magic of Kenneth Anger's classic, and in a strange way they synthesised the futuristic posturings of Glam with authentic images from the past. It was like 'living yesterday tomorrow', as Malcolm might say. But their new/old creations appealed to only the most highly clothes-literate, and the Teds on whom they had relied for custom drifted away.

MALCOLM AND VIVIENNE'S 'BONE T-SHIRT'

NEW YORK, NEW YORK

In 1973, just two years after the Angry Brigade had bombed Biba's, the New York Dolls played there. They had been featured in the previous months in the gossip columns of Andy Warhol's *Interview* magazine, and the sense of anticipation was electrifying when they stumbled on stage at the Rainbow Room. As Johnny Thunders tottered around in his platform boots waving a toy gun, the New York Dolls became the harbingers of a new pseudo-revolutionary style. The Dolls completely de-mystified the notion of the rock star. Suddenly it seemed as if anyone who had the front to do it *could* do it. Old music-biz stalwarts like Bob Harris (presenter of TV's *The Old Grey Whistle Test*) hated the very aspect that we loved, which only increased our love for the band. The music was basic, no-frills rock 'n' roll. The clothes were from thrift shops and bad. They were a cartoon version of a rock band: Johansen was more Jagger than Jagger, Thunders out-Richarded Richards, Sylvain was as pretty and diminutive as Marc Bolan, Arthur Kane looked like an enormous transvestite from suburbia, and Billy Doll was like a little poodle nodding his coiffure in time to the music.

Malcolm became obsessed with Johansen and the band, and followed them back to America where, he claims, he became their unofficial manager (a claim that is disputed by the Dolls' official manger Marty Thau as well as members of the group). What is not in question, however, is the fact that Malcolm styled the New York Dolls. In an attempt to make political iconography fashionable, and, in so doing, undermining its meaning, he pushed an incongruous Glam/Communist look on the group. They were dressed from head to toe in red vinyl, and a flag with a hammer and sickle was hung above the stages on which they played. It was Malcolm's first attempt to commodify revolution and sell it. And it was a dismal failure. Malcolm's contrived designs undermined what was intrinsic to their appeal, namely their do-it-yourself, thrift-shop exuberance. And, naturally enough, the band and Malcolm soon parted company. Nevertheless, Malcolm's association with the band and his immersion in the New York-based bohemian arty rock scene in which they operated left a profound impression on him.

At Max's, the New York club where the Dolls hung out, Richard Hell appeared with spiky hair, a leather jacket and ripped shirts with scrawled slogans, such as 'Why don't you kill me'. His songs, 'Blank Generation' for example, were about death and self-destruction. He was bored and emaciated, introverted and existential, and he epitomised the New York fashion and music scenes where something was emerging which was altogether tougher than what was happening in London . Apart from Max's, those trends were happening in the gay and particularly the S&M scene which was starting to become visible for the first time.

For some time my friend Alan Jones had been travelling to New York to visit hardcore S&M clubs, like the notorious Anvil, and he looked more scary every time he came back. Handcuffs hung from his belt and a leather jacket replaced the satin bomber jacket he wore when I first met him. Sequins were replaced with studs, platform boots with Chelsea boots. He kept me abreast of all the latest developments. There were handkerchief codes, submissive in left back pocket, dominant in right, and the colours signalled sexual preferences from yellow for golden showers to red for fist-fucking. It was the beginning of fetish wear being worn on the streets. And of course there was Warhol and his decadent 'superstars' at the Factory to which the Dolls also had access. The London scene was tame by comparison.

Inevitably the New York Dolls split up. But by the time Malcolm came back to London he had been exposed to most of the raw ingredients of what would become known as punk rock style: Situationist and King Mob rhetoric, Glam's superficiality and androgyny, Kenneth Anger's iconography, the enduring image of Richard Hell and S&M and fetish wear, plus the Warholian decadence of the Factory. But the ingredients were yet to find cohesion.

Initially it was the fetish wear that struck the crucial chord and it was sex that would be the inspiration for the next reworking of the shop. In this transition, the jukebox and a lot of the designs from Let it Rock and Too Fast To Live, Too Young To Die were carried over into the next incarnation of the shop, which was simply called SEX.

SEX

I came back to London from a trip to the USA in 1974 shortly after *The Rocky Horror Show* had married B-movie science fiction with Teddy Boy drapes, leather jackets and fetish wear. Seeing everything that was going on, I thought there might be an opening for me in the King's Road, and rented a stall in Beaufort Market with my friend Lloyd Johnson. I bought and sold old clothes that I liked but with no thought about their significance. Tim Curry was portraying a 'transvestite from transsexual Transylvania' in *The Rocky Horror Show*, Malcolm and Vivienne were running the shop at 430 King's Road, and between them was me and the Roebuck pub.

In many respects SEX was the English equivalent of the Factory in New York. It was a Mecca for 'outsiders' and 'wannabes', many of whom aspired to the status of Warhol's 'superstars'. And since Malcolm and Vivienne were a lot older (at twenty-seven and thirty-two respectively in 1974) than the menagerie of misfits who congregated in the shop, and had the responsibility of two children to clothe and feed, they began to live vicariously through their small entourage (as had Warhol).

Over in the Roebuck, Malcolm had started to play the role of Fagin to Steve Jones's artful dodger. He would boast about fencing the goods that Jones had stolen while adopting the vocal style of Ron Moody in *Oliver!* to accentuate his Jewishness in these acts of 'subversion, my dear.' Eventually, Malcolm introduced me to his protege Steve Jones and Steve's friend Paul Cook in the pub. Paul Cook remembers: 'It was handy because the number 11 bus went from Shepherd's Bush, where I lived, by the shop. Steve lived in Battersea so we met half way at World's End. We were into the Ted thing. It was the only thing that was different in 1971 or '72. Steve was up and down the King's Road all the time as he wasn't working. We were around sixteen or seventeen during the Roxy Music era. We also went to

Granny's and Alkasura, but never down the other end of King's Road. We would hang out at the shop and play records on the jukebox. I think that was Malcolm's intention – to create a scene in the shop. The first thing I bought was a pair of creepers and a zip-up top with triangular shoulders and billowing sleeves. We never stole much because we got to know Malcolm well. Although that may not have stopped Steve. He probably nicked a bit. We quickly struck up a rapport with Malcolm, being regulars through '73 to '74. We went there every weekend for a pose about. We went to the Chelsea Drug Store, Birds Nest, Rods and the Roebuck were our regular hang outs.'

Under Malcolm's patronage in the spring of 1974, Cook and Jones's group, Swankers, began rehearsing. At that time the group consisted of Wally Nightingale, Paul Cook, Glen Matlock (who worked in the shop on Saturdays) and Steve Jones on vocals. Malcolm then insisted on changing the name of the group to Q.T. Jones and the Swankers. Their slow progress and Malcolm's love for an American girl called Addie Isman propelled him back to New York, leaving instructions for Bernard Rhodes to look after the boys while he was away. Bernard Rhodes was one of the many characters who trawled the King's Road selling goods, and in 1974 he persuaded Malcolm and Vivienne to buy some glitter bomber jackets, which they hated, but which sold so well that he began printing T-shirts for the shop. Bernard: 'I brought the means of printing photographic imagery on T-shirts to Malcolm, half-tones had only just become possible with silk-screen printing.'

By 1975, after baby-sitting the group for some months, Rhodes could not see eye-to-eye with Malcolm. Rhodes was particularly upset by Malcolm's use of paedophiliac imagery. As he says, 'I wanted to do clothes for kids, not for perverts.' He refused to print a picture of a naked boy smoking a cigarette, and went off to manage the London SS, who later became the Clash. The nude boy image eventually made its way on to the first Sex Pistols T-shirt.

When Malcolm returned from New York this time, he had Sylvain's white Gibson Les Paul guitar. Like a talisman, he gave it to Steve Jones (passing on the torch, so to speak), while Wally was ejected and the group acquired a new front man called John Lydon, aka Johnny Rotten.

1975

The first thing I bought from SEX was a T-shirt left over from Too Fast To Live, Too Young To Die. It was a little grey number with soft-porn photos under gelatin, and I wore it to Ringo Starr's 1974/75 New Year's Eve party. I chopped out the coke in June's Ferrari Daytona as we sped down to Ringo's mansion in Virginia Water. When we arrived, the first person I saw was Keith Richards lying at the bottom of the staircase. Anita Pallenberg, was, at that very moment, stepping casually over the fallen rock god. But it was my SEX T-shirt which caused a fuss. Cilla Black was outraged by it. This established a mood that would prevail for the whole evening, if not the next five years.

At midnight the superstars jammed in Ringo's little studio. Keith's guitar strap kept coming undone as he swayed and struggled to keep hold of it. Elton John bashed away at a twelve-bar blues on the piano. Eric Clapton tried to keep a choppy rhythm going, while Kiki Dee sang some inane lyrics. Ronnie Wood kept getting distracted trying to help Keith hold his guitar. It was not only farcical, it was the worst racket I had ever heard. I think my unusual style – red feathered hair, winklepicker shoes, '50s drape – was overlooked, but the SEX T-shirt embarrassed June – I barely saw her all night. These people were old (some of them were in their thirties!), they were neither glamorous nor talented. I didn't belong. I was bored.

After Ringo's party I started moving away from the Chelsea set I had got to know through June, drawn to the SEX shop and the characters who would hang out where it smelt of rubber and leather, and where it was possible to see a sixty-year-old man alongside a high-class prostitute checking out rubber masks, while a sixteen-year-old boy perused the rails for T-shirts and sweaters. Vivienne struck an odd combination of the dominatrix and pantomime principal boy in leather jodhpurs, or tiny leather miniskirt with applique motorcycle badges, a thick American leather jacket, fluffy mohair sweater and little pointy booties. With her spiky, white-peroxided hair and pale skin providing a neutral background for her luscious purple lips, she was simply stunning. The only clues to her background were her over-enthusiasm (which wasn't cool) and her accent. She had grown up in the tiny village of Tintwistle, in the Peak District, and had been a schoolteacher. She had bags of 'urban' attitude, was terribly opinionated and utterly uncompromising in her beliefs and fashion sense. Mostly she lectured her young acolytes, in her quaint rural accent, about radical politics, lauding the Red Army Faction and the IRA, as well as praising the sexual politics of Wilhelm Reich. For Vivienne terrorism and the orgasm were the roads to liberation. And she had great legs. But, despite her revolutionary talk, Vivienne remained faithful to Malcolm and she didn't blow up any buildings either.

I couldn't imagine Malcolm and Vivienne apart. They seemed to share a secret. They certainly had a unique point of view. They were so sure they were right. Everything in their world was right or wrong, and people were either friends to love or foes to hate.

That kind of polarised thinking was central to Malcolm and Vivienne's creative process and they made those likes and dislikes explicit in their 'One Day You're Going To Wake Up And Realise Which Side Of The Bed You've Been Sleeping On' T-shirt (only Bernie really did it). One side listed everything they hated in British society, and the other everything they admired.

On the hate side were: 'The Liberal Party, John Betjeman, George Melly, Securicor, Honey, Harpers, Vogue, in fact all magazines that treat their readers like idiots, Bryan Ferry, Salvador Dali, The Playboy Club, Pop Stars who are thick and useless, Bernard Delfont, Arse lickers, John Osborne, Capital Radio, The Arts Council, Grey Skies, Dirty books that aren't all that dirty, The rag trade, Antiques of any sort, Bianca Jagger, The job you hate but are too scared to pack in, Chinless people, Antonia Fraser, The Archers, All those fucking saints.'

On the other side, as Malcolm's old art-school buddy, Fred Vermorel, puts it, 'was everything that gave us hope': 'Eddie Cochrane, Christine Keeler, Susan 6022509, Brazil, Coffee bars that sell whisky under the counter, Valerie Solanas, Buenaventura Durruti, Archie Shepp, Olympia Press, Lenny Bruce, Joe Orton, Zoot suits and dreadlocks, Simone de Beauvoir, Dashiell Hammett, Alex Trocchi, Marianne Faithful, Imagination. '

Malcolm and Vivienne's blind belief in their own project's righteousness led them to become increasingly ambitious as their confidence developed.

IT WASN'T CALLED PUNK

When Alan Jones (from whom I had first learned about the New York S&M scene) started working in the shop, he began decking himself out from head to toe in SEX clothes. One of the shop's T-shirts particularly appealed to his bizarre taste. Emblazoned on the front was a print of two cowboys with their cocks out by the gay artist Tom of Finland, along with the memorable slogan:
'Ello Joe, been anywhere lately?'
'Nah, it's all played aht Bill
'Gettin too straight'

Alan's new style incensed people even more than his previous one, and in June 1975 he was arrested in Piccadilly and charged with gross indecency for wearing the nude cowboy T-shirt (he seemed terribly heroic to me). On the evening of his arrest I went to discuss his case with Malcolm, Vivienne and Gene Krell (then owner of Granny Takes a Trip) at the Portobello Hotel, where Alan also worked as the receptionist. At the meeting Malcolm and Vivienne were most emphatic about Alan's right to wear whatever he wanted. And since it was one of their designs that had landed him in trouble, they promised to support him by finding him a lawyer and paying for his case. This was to be an ideological battle and they intended to be on the front line with Alan in court. But they didn't turn up at the hearing and Alan, who couldn't afford to contest the charges, was forced to plead guilty and was fined. Alan was hurt by the snub, but, unperturbed, he continued wearing Malcolm and Vivienne's clothes through 1975 and into 1977.

At the end of 1975 business at my stall was dreadful. My problems were compounded when June caught me playing around with Miss Cinderella, the notorious LA groupie and wife of John Cale, a founding member of the Velvet Underground. Bang went the Ferrari – June went off to Brazil. At the beginning of 1976 I was left high-

and-dry and broke. Malcolm, Vivienne and Chrissie Hynde were hanging around the house I had moved into with some hippie drug-smugglers in Richmond, and, to the horror of my house-mates, Jordan, the outrageous shop assistant from SEX, sometimes stayed overnight. We spent a lot of time in each other's company, going to parties and restaurants together, and drinking a great deal. It was during one drunken conversation that we decided to start a club. Malcolm was also keen for me to see 'his' group and he invited me to one of the Sex Pistols gigs. I had little hope that the band he referred to as 'the new Bay City Rollers' would be to my taste. Nevertheless, in January 1976, more to spend some time with Vivienne than anything else, I went to see the Sex Pistols perform at the Marquee.

THE NEW BAY CITY ROLLERS

In January 1976, Vivienne, Chrissie Hynde and Malcolm picked me up from the house in Richmond and we all travelled up to Soho in Viv's puke-green Mini. When we arrived the group was already playing. There were very few punters, and even fewer who were interested in the Sex Pistols. Most of the small crowd were there to see Eddie and the Hot Rods whom the Sex Pistols were supporting.

I was struck by the singer's extraordinary appearance. The musicians were in SEX clothes, which was novel and impressive, except for John who had customised his own. They were cruder than Malcolm and Vivienne's creations, but their idiosyncrasy more than made up for what they lacked in craftsmanship. His style was reminiscent of Old Steptoe (I found out later that *Steptoe and Son* was one of his favourite TV shows). A pink school blazer had been customised with safety pins and chains, and he wore an old red pullover which was ripped and far too small. When he took it off he revealed a yellow Pink Floyd T-shirt on which he had scrawled 'I Hate'. His jeans were baggy, thereby completely desexualising the trousers that had been worn skin tight for as long as I could remember. His face was so ugly it was beautiful: like the face of a psychotic boy.

Rotten's performance reminded me of Iggy Pop, whom I had seen at the King's Cross Cinema in 1972 when he ran across the audience, spat in a girl's face and fell in the orchestra pit (a similar performance in America inspired Bowie to re-evaluate his act in 1969). Yet he was as ungainly as pub rocker/polio victim Ian Dury whose group Kilburn and the Highroads was managed by Tommy Roberts of Mr Freedom. Claiming he had always wanted to see his group play, Rotten sat in the audience and sang, while Steve Jones, Glen Matlock and Paul Cook struck classic rock 'n' roll poses. Out of frustration or, perhaps, to divert attention from his inability to sing, Rotten picked up chairs and threw them across the dance floor. He finished the set by smashing the microphone. It struck me that the Sex Pistols were more like performance art than conventional rock and roll. Yet Rotten's spontaneous antics were not the contrived theatrics of David Bowie and Bryan Ferry. The Sex Pistols were the real thing. Whether Malcolm recognised it or not, and he seemed at that time not to recognise it, the Sex Pistols were anything but the new Bay City Rollers.

The delinquents who made up the group concentrated many of the interesting raw ingredients that were floating around in the culture into a powerful unified whole. But it was Rotten's angst-ridden asexuality and his penchant for customising his own clothes which provided the real focus for the group. He was anti-music, anti-fashion, anti-art, anti-sex, anti-world. It was an aesthetic master stroke. Johnny Rotten's whole being screamed, 'NO!'

Ironically, the Sex Pistols were a lot tighter and more interesting musically than the superstars I had seen jamming at Ringo Starr's house, and in their company no one ignored me because of the way I looked, quite the opposite, in fact. I felt at home. I wasn't bored.

For so long you had had to be gay, or at least give the impression of being bisexual, to be fashionable. Faking had become a terrible strain, so the laddishness of the Sex Pistols and the enigmatic style of Johnny Rotten along with the coded messages in SEX clothing were irresistible to me. Anyway business was terrible, I had nothing to lose and at the beginning of 1976 I did a moonlight flit from my stall to work with the Sex Pistols with Malcolm, and my brother Ray joined me. In the late 1960s, Ray had worked as a photographer for the radical underground papers, *Frendz*, *Oz* and *International Times*. Although he had developed relationships with many of the rock stars of the period (including Marc Bolan and David Bowie), they dropped him when they became famous. He was in semi-retirement and disillusioned when he began taking pictures of the Sex Pistols and their entourage. With my brother and me, the group of misfits who would contribute to the Sex Pistols' notoriety and punk rock ideology was beginning to cohere.

In 1976 music was increasingly technologically driven, with highly produced disco records and the work of the seminal German techno band Kraftwerk. By this time, Bowie had killed off his rock-star alter ego Ziggy, and both these musical forms were influencing his work. An alternative was provided by long-haired Californian rock groups singing about a distant lifestyle. From the UK there was also the overblown music of tax exiles like Mick Jagger and Rod Stewart, and the attempt to reinvent rhythm-and-blues by new groups on the pub-rock circuit. In contrast, the Sex Pistols adopted an almost Luddite approach to music-making, were wholly British and highly critical of contemporary culture. Those aspects were very appealing to me and a few other fashion victims. It was as if, in all the technical sophistication, soft rock and nostalgia for an outmoded musical form, something important had been forgotten, and in the Pistols we were going back to the roots of the thing.

Before the global corporatisation of pop music by MTV and the establishment of fashion bibles like *The Face* in the '80s, youth culture was marginal. We owned it and, with no regard for 'authenticity', we manipulated it with an irreverence previously unheard of. Although the 1967 summer of love was still hanging over us, the smart hippies had abandoned their principles and were making money, and long hair, dope-smoking and most of the other features of hippiedom were no longer shocking. It was natural, therefore, to develop a credo of hate.

Pre-AIDS, when the most serious sexually transmitted diseases could be cured with a course of penicillin, punk was a cage to run wild in.

Nils Stevenson, August 1998

PUNK ~~Romanticism~~ is the primitive, the untutored, it is youth, life,...but it is also pallor, fever, disease, decadence,... the Dance of Death, indeed Death itself.... It is the confused teeming fullness and richness of life,...turbulence, violence, conflict, chaos, but it is also peace.... It is the strange, the exotic, the grotesque,...the irrational, the unutterable....

Isaiah Berlin, *The Roots of Romanticism*, 1965

Anarchy Tour Flag
Jamie Reid, Ray Stevenson

THE PUNK ARISTOCRACY
Colour photographs

Sex Pistols

Rotten

Debbie, Siouxsie and Steve Severin

Debbie and Sue Catwoman

Sharon and Simon

Walter Lure and Johnny Thunders

Siouxsie and Jordan

Nils

The Clash

Slits

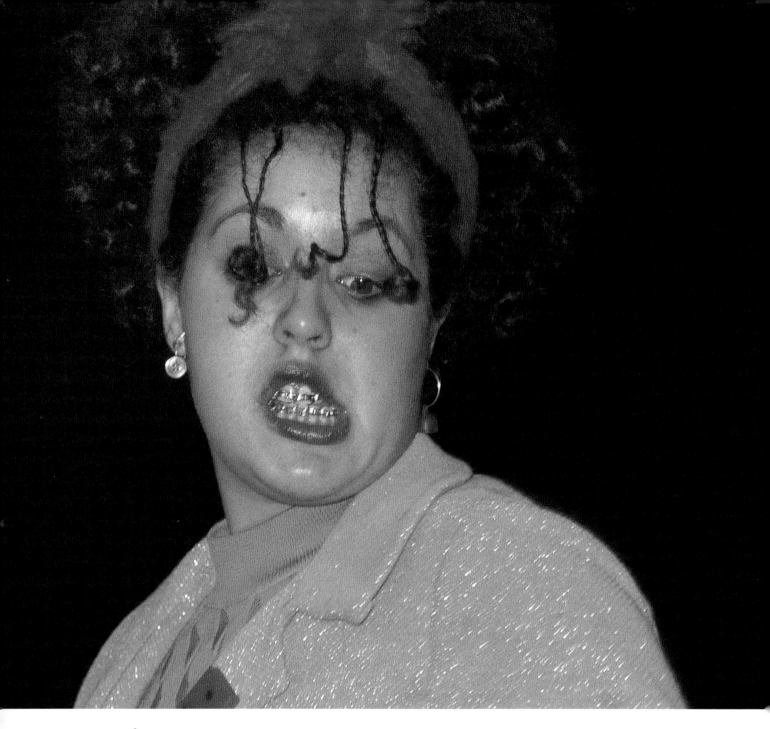

Poly Styrene

Margret

Steve Jones
and Jamie Reid

Glen Matlock
and Paul Cook

Glen Matlock
and Paul Cook

Sid

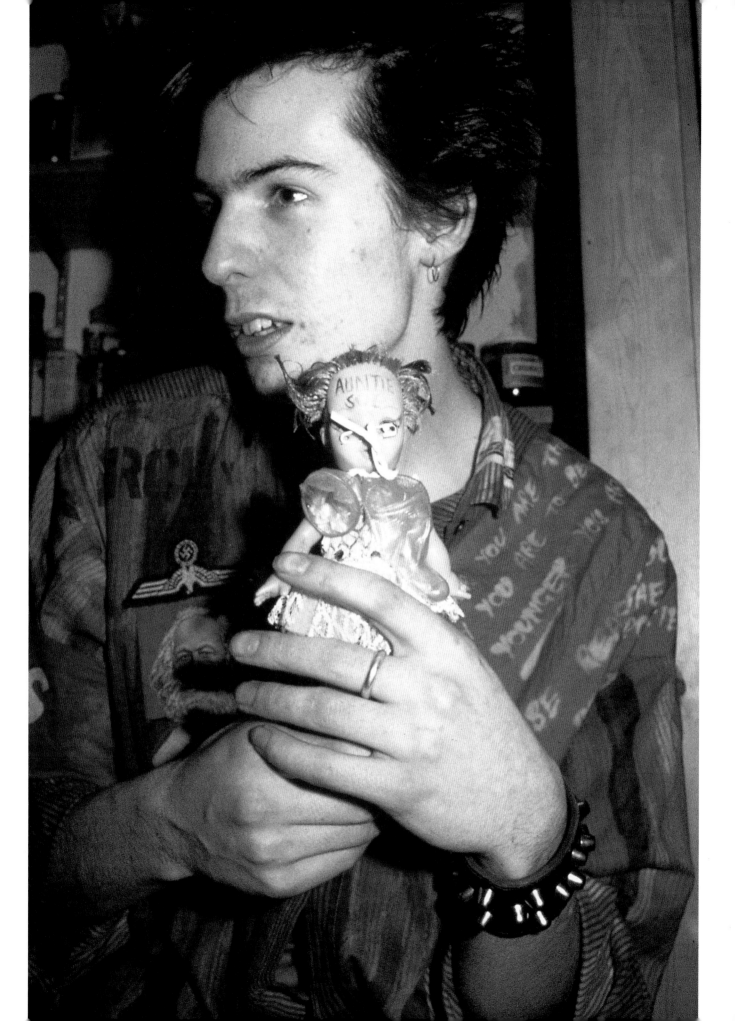

Rotten and McLaren

Shepherd's bush roundabout:
Jamie Reid

I am a person who is totally comfortable with myself, I have been this way from very early on in my childhood having very clear ideas as to how I want to look. This confidence allows me to be me without the need for others to sanction it. My earliest feelings of this self awareness was at the age of seven and it is therefore obvious that I was meant to be in these photos you see, I suppose born to it and it felt like a homecoming. I was totally at ease with my 'fame' if you like and this unassailable power that people saw in me. There is no why or how, it was meant to happen. This is not the stuff of nostalgia to be diluted and perverted by time, it was unique and without restrictions. The period depicted in this book is my time.

Jordan

JORDAN, 1998

JORDAN AND POLICE

A DIARY OF
THE PUNK YEARS
1976–79

EL PARADISE club

BREWER ST W1
SUNDAY APRIL 4TH
7PM-2AM

JOHNNY ROTTEN, ST ALBANS, 19 FEBRUARY

19 FEBRUARY

Malcolm and I are getting shows on the pub-and-college circuits for the Sex Pistols. I'm also designing flyers with Helen Wellington-Lloyd and driving the group to gigs. Get Ray to come up to St Albans College of Art for his first photo-shoot of the group.

1 APRIL

Hassling with a Maltese character called Vincent for El Paradise strip club. Track him down to a Soho gambling club. Malcolm knocks on the door and, as it opens, he pushes me inside a small smoky room with card tables.

THE SEX PISTOLS, EL PARADISE STRIP CLUB, SOHO, 4 APRIL

A group of very pissed-off heavy bastards are not amused by this
interruption. I think I am going to get my head kicked in. Vincent
obviously just wants to diffuse this embarrassing situation. He jostles
me out of the room and agrees to £90 rent for the club. Malcolm later
complains that it is extortionate and that I am useless.

Everything comes off without a hitch. We don't have a liquor licence,
but Jordan and Michael Collins (who both work in SEX) sell punch
anyway. Alan Jones is on the door looking amazing in a leather mask and
Perv T-shirt. I have to give some chubby stripper a few quid because
she was booked to perform by Vincent. While she does her strip, there
are screams and howls of derision from the small excitable audience.
The Pistols are really manic when they eventually get on the small
stage, though Rotten calms down when Vincent and his henchmen arrive
to check on the proceedings. It's a great success. But Malcolm claims
we haven't made a profit. Total take £240, £90 of which goes for rental.
I wonder where the rest went?

4 APRIL

5 APRIL

Malcolm has left Vivienne and moved in with Helen in Bell Street – her flat is now our office. Helen and Malcolm met in 1968 at Goldsmiths Art College, and later they had a brief fling. Helen then became involved in the Soho scene, nurturing relationships with working girls and turning the odd trick herself.

HELEN WELLINGTON-LLOYD, BELL STREET, APRIL

I always had a negative self conscious image of myself.
But being part of an outrageous clique made me feel secure.
Nobody had dressed like us before so Plebs couldn't categorise me, which made it possible for me to be myself. I felt liberated and thats when I started to live.
For a time I was unaware of the negative side of being a freak Plebs varded me because of what I was wearing not because of my height I became Threatening. —
It was an artistic experience that is hard to define.
It was like a happening, —
an exploration, There was no 'formula. It was BONA!

Helen Wellington-Lloyd

HELEN WELLINGTON-LLOYD, 1997

CHRISSIE HYNDE, THE ANTICHRIST AND JESUS, THE NASHVILLE, 6 APRIL

6 APRIL

Jesus has been dancing in the nude at hippie concerts for years. His arrival in a dog collar (the canine variety) is quite a surprise.

15 APRIL

Malcolm and I visit John Curd the promoter re Pistols supporting the Ramones at the Roundhouse. Curd (a big man) throws us down the stairs after Malcolm calls him an arsehole for not liking the Pistols. Later Malcolm chastises me for not sticking up for myself.

STEVE, ROTTEN, GLEN, PAUL, MALCOLM AND NILS, MAJESTIC STUDIOS, 12 MAY

Sex Pistols' recording session with Chris Spedding at Majestic Studios. What a mess. Spedding's got an extraordinary German girlfriend – Nora. In the evening Rotten hacks off my hair with a razor blade. My new look makes people step out of my way in the street, but Vivienne hates it.

12 MAY

Chrissie Hynde wants me to play guitar in a group she hopes to form called the Mark Hunt Band.

2 JULY

We've done a deal with Roger Austin, the manager of the Screen on the Green cinema in Islington. Take over the cinema after the movies have finished. The Pistols are starting to attract an interesting collection of freaks who show up on mass tonight. The bill comprises the Buzzcocks, Clash (on the condition that they build a stage) and Pistols, plus Malcolm's favourite film 'Scorpio Rising'. I can't help thinking most of the punters would have preferred a more mainstream stockings-and-swastika movie like 'Cabaret', since the style of most of them combines elements of Glam, 'Clockwork Orange', 'Cabaret' and 'The Rocky Horror Show'. Steve Jones always gets very nervous and spews up before he goes on stage. Tonight he vomits into Roger's filing cabinet.

29 AUGUST

STEVE SEVERIN, SIOUXSIE AND DEBBIE, SCREEN ON THE GREEN, 29 AUGUST

Soho, 1976 taking a turn off Oxford St., away from the heckling & jeckling real-world War II relics and into the outer spaces teen-angst faces and sour deafening sounds of rock 'n' roll. That inner space... a mind loses its moorings. What's the date again? (it's so tense in here) 1996? or twenty years on? is this a concert or a moonage daydream riot going on? paradise or el paradise? Johnny turns his back... oh! now! that is so cool... (there had been rumours, of course, nothing certain, but the suggestion of a new violence). Musicians jerk rigid & spiked in a situationist canvas of hard-edged misshapen tatters, grim reapers masquerade as clean-cut edwardian malchicks, a smoky impending doom...

.... feeling the music resounding, cutting the air like flying glass, rock 'n' roll subverted into the demonic electronic supersonic ap-ap. apocalypse by a careering imploding deathwish upon such stars lofi- or lowlife who can tell? wailing stooge-time strings, velvet/viscous, vibrato/sidvicious or entropic & sonic (& more)... splintered into whirls & whorls of decaying sound. gripped/slipped/liplined & hipper than thou to diving, high-rising slabs & fissures of pure amplified rage — squirming, spitting tormenting (oh the notes will spell out the scene) fantasising; eulogising; echoes of magic golden year moments become real presences... dreamworld & realworld downloaded with images.

(of a fear & dread & world of sunken dreams?)

Bisexual & transexual fragments recharged and renourished to pan, scan the limits of sensational rocky horror... trails of blood, crossing barriers & minds. Saturday nite at the Roxy, the Screen, the 100... your fantasies realised & are they still? & is this the end? the bitter end? (or the beginning? &, so help me, so many questions? & are the answers naked to the eye — or ear? or are they undiscovered?

Steven Severin   1st June 1997

(liberally adapted from Simon Puxley's liner notes to the first Roxy Music album.)

STEVE SEVERIN, 1997

ARRIVAL IN PARIS, 3 SEPTEMBER

3–4 SEPTEMBER

Fly to Paris to play the opening night of a new disco called Le Chalet du Lac (a most inappropriate venue). Billy Idol, Siouxsie, Steve Severin and another Bromley boy, Simon Barker, come over in Billy's van. Vivienne and Jordan, journalists Caroline Coon and Jonh Ingham, who are pushing the Pistols in Sounds and NME, turn up as well.

VIVIENNE, ROTTEN AND JORDAN, SNAX DELUXE FOYER, 3 SEPTEMBER

Three F's - Form, Fucking and Function. Malcolm and Vivienne's new and best creation, the Bondage Suit, really expresses Rotten's confused sexuality. Naturally he customises the suit they give him for the French trip and looks stunning.

This trip is a welcome break from touring the provinces and it's a thrill to hang out at Jean-Paul Sartre's favourite café as part of a new English philosophical movement. Malcolm often fancies himself as a bit of an Existentialist. Steve Jones, on the other hand, is the English Jean Genet, the type who gets a hard-on during a burglary.

JOHNNY ROTTEN, PARIS, 4 SEPTEMBER

JONH INGHAM, BACKSTAGE, CHALET DU LAC

NILS, ROTTEN AND CAROLINE COON, DEUX MAGOTS CAFÉ, PARIS, 4 SEPTEMBER

1976

A massive crowd congregates outside the club. Police arrive, and the situation rapidly turns into mayhem as it gets dark. Inside there's plenty of aggro directed at Siouxsie, whose swastika and pert bare breasts provoke a furore from French patriots. I have to hide her away backstage. The Pistols' performance itself is greeted with bewilderment.

ROTTEN, ON STAGE, CHALET DU LAC

SIOUXSIE BACKSTAGE WITH JONH INGHAM, SEVERIN AND ROTTEN

1976

6 SEPTEMBER

In England it's back to the same old grind – 100 Club and dates up north, shuttling the group out of pub gigs where Rotten's antics often wind up the crowd to such an extent that I am forced to demand police escorts to nasty bed-and-breakfasts, where Steve finds the necessity to choose between cornflakes or grapefruit segments for breakfast hilarious, and Rotten moans about nylon sheets.

MALCOLM MCLAREN

CLASH MANAGER, BERNARD RHODES, WITH OLD GREY WHISTLE TEST PRESENTER BOB HARRIS, DINGWALLS

DEBBIE JUVENILE, BILLY IDOL, SIOUXSIE, AND PETER FENTON, 100 CLUB

50

SIOUXSIE

THE CLASH

SIMON

LINDA

CELIA

SIOUXSIE AND MARCO

CELIA

T.V. SMITH AND GAYE ADVERT

SHARON

FAN

MATLOCK AND FRIEND

FANS

FROM RAY'S CONTACT SHEETS, 100 CLUB, SEPTEMBER

Glen's always trolling around with his girlfriend Celia. He likes the Beatles. Jonesy stays in Richmond and nicks some jewellery from the hippies I share the house with, so I have to move into the stinking rehearsal studio in Denmark Street with a fucking kleptomaniac.

9 SEPTEMBER

Ray's old friend Bob Harris of 'The Old Grey Whistle Test' (the only TV programme that offers an alternative to 'Top of the Pops'), hated everything I loved, from Roxy Music to the New York Dolls. His time is up because of people like us and Bernard (who's managing the Clash).

10 SEPTEMBER

WHEN BRYAN FERRY DID HIS G.I. LOOK, IT WAS LIKE ELVIS GOING INTO THE ARMY. THERE WAS NO-ONE TO LOOK TO FOR GUIDANCE YOU HAD TO FIND "IT" YOURSELF.

AS I HAD SUSPECTED FOR A LONG TIME "IT" WAS BEGINING TO HAPPEN AT THE WRONG END OF THE KINGS RD AT THE SHOP.

WHAT "IT" WAS, AND WHAT "IT" WOULD BECOME, I HAD NO IDEA, BUT I KNEW "IT" LOOKED GOOD AND "IT" FELT GOOD AND BEST OF ALL THE REST OF THE WORLD HATED "IT".

I LOVED "IT"

MARCO

8/6/97

MARCO PIRRONI, 1997

15 SEPTEMBER

The Pistols' gigs at the 100 Club have become wonderful, intimate events. Someone in a music paper wrote that you could piss in the toilets next to current stars like Rotten, whereas Mick Jagger and his ilk are little more than specks on the stages of the world's arenas. The term 'punk' is starting to be applied to us. Malcolm prefers New Wave in deference to his favourite French movies from the '60s, or even worse, 'dole-queue rock'. I prefer punk, but I fear the consequences of being categorised and subsequently, stereotyped.

21 SEPTEMBER

Siouxsie and the Banshees take to the stage at the 100 Club Punk Festival for their first-ever performance. Siouxsie who can't sing, Steve Severin who can't play bass, Marco Pirroni who can play guitar and Sid Vicious who can't play drums, make a wonderful racket for about fifteen minutes, as Siouxsie shouts lyrics from the Lord's Prayer, 'Twist and Shout', 'Knocking On Heaven's Door', and 'Deutschland, Deutschland Über Alles', while Marco pulls out a catalogue of familiar riffs. It reminds me of Yoko Ono's album 'Fly'. Everyone hates them. I want to manage them. Bernard won't let the Banshees use the Clash's equipment because of Sid and Siouxsie's swastikas. This incenses Sid who berates Bernard from the stage, calling him a 'tight old Jew'.

Subway Sect perform a very subdued set, but Malcolm thinks they are a better bet than Siouxsie.

23 SEPTEMBER

Jonesy and I visit Sid in Ashford Remand Centre where he was taken after his arrest for allegedly throwing a glass and partially blinding a young girl on the second night of the 100 Club Punk Festival. We were doing an out-of-town date, so we weren't there when the incident happened. Sid claims he didn't do it.

24 SEPTEMBER

Over in Rotten's bedroom at his parents' council flat in Finsbury Park it is the sophisticated sounds of Captain Beefheart and Can. Rots and I also go to listen to reggae at the Q Club in Praed Street where we are the only white faces, or to his other favourite hangout the Black Cap in Camden, where drag acts mime to Judy Garland and Diana Ross.

25 SEPTEMBER

So many girls around, it's got to the point where shagging is like shaking hands. It seems impolite to refuse anyone.

29 SEPTEMBER

Go to clap clinic.

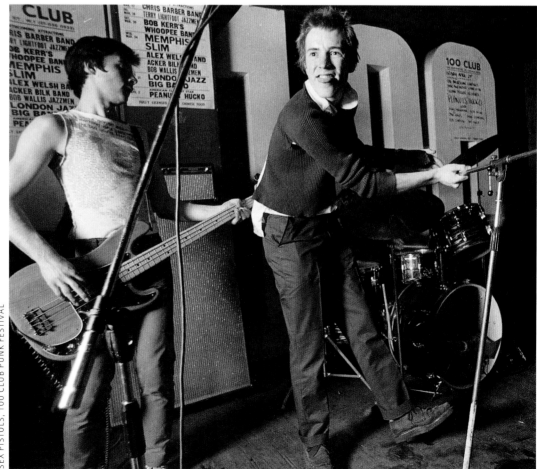

SEX PISTOLS, 100 CLUB PUNK FESTIVAL

When we're really starving, Steve and I walk from Denmark Street over to Paul Cook's parents' house in Hammersmith. Paul likes Roxy Music, Sparks and the Faces. Trying to get him to leave his job at Watney's brewery.

It's rumoured that Ari Up's mum, Nora (Chris Spedding's ex), is the billionaire heiress of a German newspaper baron. When Steve isn't with her, he's great fun. He's not only a kleptomaniac, he's an absolute sex fiend. But the Denmark Street studio where we live is a fucking tip. The toilet in a small courtyard outside is disgusting and I try not to use it. There's no bathroom or kitchen, just a hot plate next to a sink in the living-quarters above the rehearsal studio. We listen to the mice running around at night, and the damp cork walls make everything – clothes, equipment – smell distinctly corky. I'm starting to appreciate Steve's special talent – if he couldn't nick food we would starve. But I'm getting sick of baked beans. Steve's showing an interest in reading so he can read about the band in the music papers.

Lots of girls, like Paul's new girfriend Kay, have pulled their old school blazers out of the closet, and are wearing St Trinian's outfits.

NORA WITH STEVE JONES, DINGWALLS

PAUL COOK AND KAY, 100 CLUB

SUE CATWOMAN

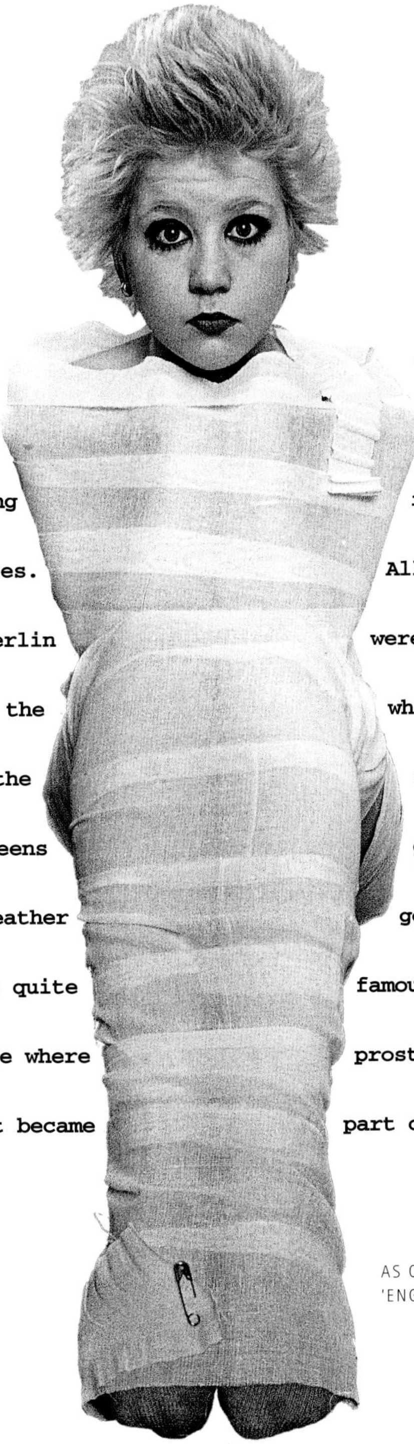

People think that the early days of Punk were all banging along at Sex Pistol gigs. But for me it was camping it up down Park Lane with a gang of trannies. All my friends John, Blanche, Tracey, Berlin were on the game. Linda of course was on the whipping sessions. It was all in Park Lane: it was the most outrageous place in the world. All these queens going around in Punk gear and black leather going 'Ooooooh!' They actually became quite famous down there; it got to the stage where prostitution wasn't that bad a thing to do. It became part of the new London.

DEBBIE IN BANDAGE BONDAGE

DEBBIE JUVENILE
AS QUOTED BY JON SAVAGE IN
'ENGLAND'S DREAMING', 1991

I've started to see a lot of little Debbie, who'll turn 16 any day now. | 4 OCTOBER

Sue Catwoman is one of the most extraordinary-looking girls around. Ray tells me she has a passion for criminals. Like the Bromley Contingent, she's from the suburbs. | 5 OCTOBER

SID, NILS AND LINDA, AT LINDA'S FLAT

Staying at a dominatrix called Linda's flat, opposite Scotland Yard, a stone's throw from Buckingham Palace and not far from the Houses of Parliament. At her work premises in Earls Court she entertains MPs and celebrities, and she is much admired in the Sex Pistols' camp for her anecdotes about whipping the rich and famous. She is, with delicious irony, paid to enslave our enslavers. There is fur wrapped around the entrance to her bedroom to make it look like a giant pussy. Usually a girl to shag there. Get Ray to do a photo session with the Pistols' most ardent fans at Linda's for our own newspaper. Been doing tons of sulphate. The inside of my mouth feels raw and my nerves are getting frayed. There are all sorts of problems with the band and we are always blamed for causing trouble, and Malcolm whines constantly about how he should be spending more time in his shop where the money is.

1976

Sid and John stay at Linda's now and then. Jonesy comes over too, when he's not with Nora. The Bromley Contingent and Adam Ant stay as well. Sometimes it's so crowded, I have to share the bed with Sid who smells. His favourite group is Abba.

I've been lumped in with the Bromley Contingent by the press, though I've never been near Bromley. That's not quite true – we went to Berlin's fetish party – bit of an orgy. Siouxsie's having a thing with Severin, but Cookie steamed in anyway. Steve got hold of Tracey, and I met a Ted girl. Glen and Celia were outraged and left.

At Louise's, the dyke club in Soho, the music is all disco, like George McCray, Dr Alimontado's 'Cocaine' and Hughes Corporation. Every night ends with Maurice Chevalier's 'Every Little Breeze Seems to Whisper Louise'. After signing to EMI, we truck down to Louise's to celebrate. Fucking pissed off that there's no provision for me in the management contract. Malcolm gives me an ultimatum – I can stay on as a roadie or he will pay me off after the Anarchy in the UK tour: £300. I don't want to leave the group, but I'll sneak Siouxsie and guitarist Peter Fenton, into the Pistols' studio to rehearse while we're away on the tour.

DEBBIE, SIOUXSIE, PHILLIP SALON AND MALCOLM, AT LOUISE'S, 9 OCTOBER

We came together at the time of GLAM ROCK. It was the BOWIE/ROXY part of Glam we identified with. Yes we liked T.REX, THE SWEET GARY GLITTER etc but we laughed at, and not with, their (tacky) sense of style + taste.

Dissolution set in when BOWIE disappeared to Berlin and FERRY started wearing tuxedos.

Fortunately for us Londoners things were happening in New York. (Things always seem more exciting when they come from a foreign place, especially the U.S.). TELEVISION, RICHARD HELL and most importantly THE NEW YORK DOLLS. They were just like us. They used thrift shops, imagination, camp and rock 'n' roll and merged it into their own (life)style. The Dolls showed that anyone (who looked glamorous enough) could become rock stars. Musicianship was secondary. We loved them and were inspired by them.

We knew that when we went out people would stare at our dress or our multi coloured hair. So what if they laughed or shouted out. If they did was because they didn't understand. We looked fucking brilliant - and if the rest of Joe public couldn't see that what did we care? Some journalists - who gave us the collective name of the BROMLEY CONTINGENT - called us street theatre. What an Insult!

The only clubs that accepted the way we dressed were gay clubs. Unfortunately at that time it was the height of fashion to go round claiming to be gay, or at least bisexual. The gay clubs such as RODS, SHAGARAMA and the SOMBRERO, were the most desired places in London to get into. As a result the doormen became stricter + stricter on who they let in. Fashion wise sometimes

we were a little too avant garde, i.e. before fashion, even for the gay clubs. The most important of all these gay clubs was BANGS. This club was was every Monday night + held over two thousand people. Even so such was its popularity that it soon became members only and we used to have to ask members to take us in with them. Invariably we failed + ended up in a seedy club called the REGENCY. Here we mixed with prostitutes, rent boys, pimps and drag queens etc and felt completely at ease. These people all had their own style — especially the drag queens and we had some great nights there.

This led us to discover a little known lesbian club in SOHO called LOUISES. Frequented by prostitutes and, on our first night there, ladies Wimbledon tennis players. It was here in LOUISES that the hardcore of the LONDON PUNK scene met by night.   Simon Barker

VIVIENNE ON STAGE WITH THE SEX PISTOLS, NOTRE DAME HALL, LEICESTER SQUARE, 15 OCTOBER

15 OCTOBER

Malcolm's moved back with Vivienne, though she's around less now. But when she does turn up she is very enthusiastic about everything. I guess it's because she's stuck in Clapham the rest of the time.

18 OCTOBER

We have proper offices in Dryden Chambers off Oxford Street. Jamie Reid's now doing all the graphics, and his girlfriend, Sophie Richmond, has replaced Helen, giving the impression that the Sex Pistols' management company, Glitterbest, is an organised operation. Ha, ha.

20 OCTOBER

The Damned play at Eater's school in Finchley. The audience, who before were as interesting as the action on stage, are now invading the stage. The distance between spectator and performer is breaking down.

30 NOVEMBER

Malcolm and Vivienne are renaming the shop Seditionaries. It will look like a cross between a solicitor's office and a massage parlour, with frosted windows. Inside will be a huge photo of Dresden after the bombing, another of an upside-down Eros, and a hole punched in the ceiling.

ROB COLLINS, SECOND FROM RIGHT, DAMNED GIG, MANOR HILL SCHOOL, FINCHLEY

1976 - 15 YEARS OLD

A (NO) FUTURE MOULDED BY PARENT'S ASPIRATIONS, A DEAD
END GOVERNMENT AND A LACK OF SELF CONFIDENCE
TRANSFORMED OVERNIGHT TO A FUTURE CONTROLLED BY THE
INDIVIDUAL. 'PUNK' WAS AN OPENING OF THE CONSCIOUSNESS,
A WAY OF DEALING WITH LIFE. A KICK-START TO WHAT WAS
POSSIBLE. A CRASH COURSE IN MUSIC, SEX, DRUGS,
ALCOHOL, ART, POLITICS AND CULTURE. NO RULES —
EVERYTHING WAS AND STILL IS POSSIBLE. IT'S FOOTPRINT
HAS NEVER LEFT

28/2/98 - 11.50 PM

ROB COLLINS, 1998

65

1 DECEMBER

Send the EMI limo to pick up the Heartbreakers who fly in from New York to support the Pistols on the Anarchy tour. The same evening, the Pistols appear on the Today programme on TV, presented by Bill Grundy:

Siouxsie to Grundy: I've always wanted to meet you …

Grundy: We'll meet afterwards, shall we?

Steve Jones: You dirty sod. You dirty old man!

Grundy: Well keep going chief, keep going. Go on, you've got another ten seconds. Say something outrageous.

Steve: You dirty bastard!

Grundy: Go on again!

Steve: You dirty fucker!

Grundy: What a clever boy!

Steve: You fucking rotter!

I'm at a rehearsal studio in Harlesden preparing for the Anarchy tour, but Malcolm phones me afterwards, completely freaked out. He thinks the group have blown it and will be thrown off EMI. It's really funny.

2 DECEMBER

Amazing response from the national press: the story's on every front page and news bulletin. We're no longer enigmatic freaks, we're suddenly despised 'punks'. People used to get out of my way, but they now barge me off the pavement. Malcolm is fuelling the animosity between Teds and punks – there are running battles in the King's Road, and Chelsea football hooligans smash the windows of the shop on Saturdays.

3 DECEMBER

Jamie's graphics have come on a treat, and Ray has teamed up with him to produce the Anarchy flag and the Anarchy in the UK newspaper. But the style hasn't changed much since Helen and I sat around Bell Street cutting up newspapers, though it's more overtly Situationist now.

4 DECEMBER   The Anarchy in the UK Tour is the road to nowhere. All but three gigs out of nineteen scheduled are cancelled after the Grundy incident. Nevertheless we're travelling around the country stirring up publicity with three other groups who are not being allowed to play. The Damned travel separately and stay in different hotels. But the tour has given me the opportunity to smuggle Siouxsie and her new Banshees into the Pistols' studio while we are away.

6 DECEMBER   Malcolm has pushed himself into the limelight and is now conducting interviews on behalf of the group. He's in his element, feigning outrage about the way the Sex Pistols are being persecuted.

THE SEX PISTOLS, THE CLASH AND THE HEARTBREAKERS ON THE ANARCHY TOUR BUS

MALCOLM CONDUCTING TV INTERVIEW, ANARCHY TOUR

We all wait around all the time to find out if gigs are on or not, while Malcolm and the Pistols take meetings and conduct interviews.

7 DECEMBER

THE HEARTBREAKERS, THE CLASH AND THE DAMNED, WAITING AROUND, ANARCHY TOUR

8 DECEMBER   Generally the equipment goes up in the morning and comes down in the afternoon. Then it's back to rearrange furniture.

9 DECEMBER   The roadies trash Bernard's room and shit in his bed. I have a terrible fight with Rotten in the hotel room we're sharing. After the dust settles he says he really respects me now. What working-class bullshit is this?

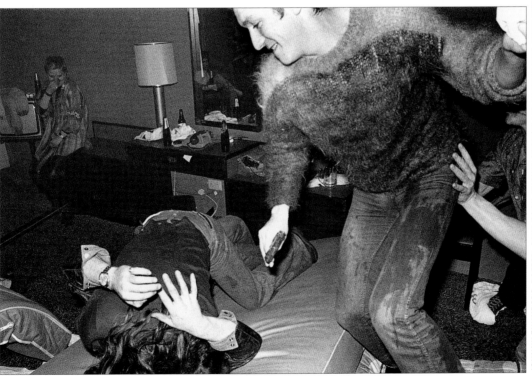

JOHNNY THUNDERS, ROTTEN, PAUL COOK, MICKEY FOOT (CLASH SOUNDMAN), MICK JONES AND ROADIES TRASH BERNARD RHODES'S ROOM

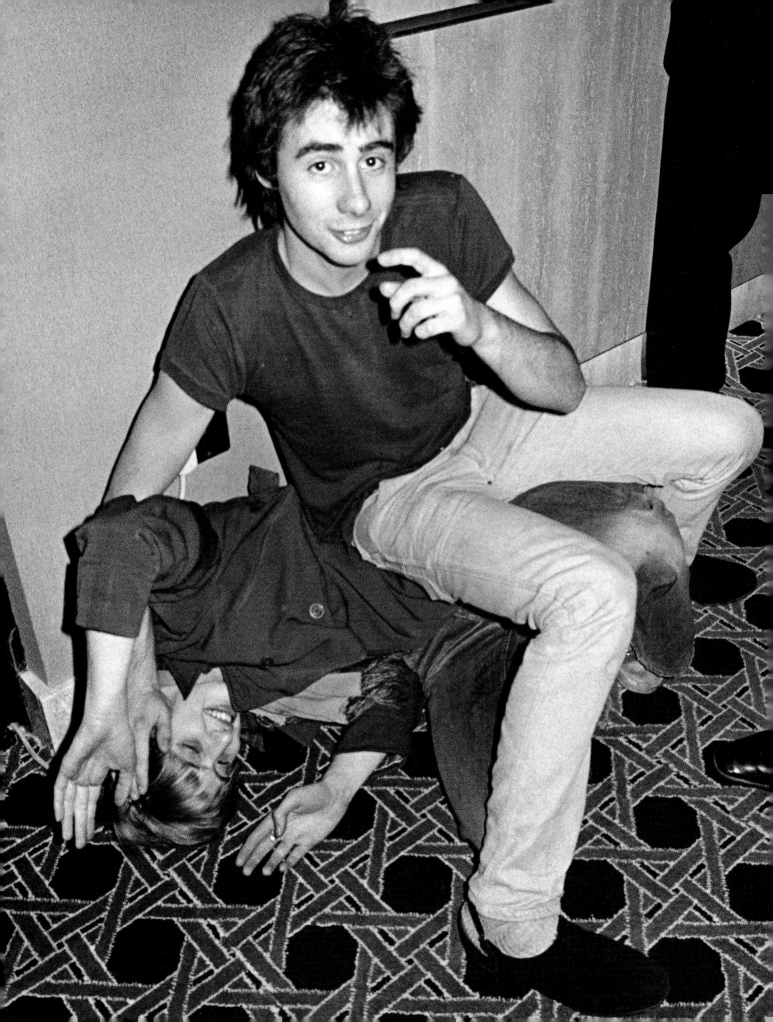

Sophie, Malcolm's secretary, comes on the road for a few days but it is a little too much for her, and she soon splits back to London.

We've never really got along with the Clash, but this tour has built some bridges. Glen has become particularly friendly with Mick Jones, and if it weren't for Bernie, I would starve – he always makes sure there's some scraps for me when I've sorted out the equipment after the cancelled gigs. Everyone loved the Heartbreakers immediately – Nolan and Thunders' pedigrees are immaculate coming from the New York Dolls, and their manager Leee Black Childers used to work for Bowie.

JOE STRUMMER AND PAUL SIMONON OF THE CLASH

OPPOSITE: GLEN MATLOCK AND SOPHIE RICHMOND

DEBBIE AND TRACEY O'KEEFE WITH MICK JONES OF THE CLASH

12 DECEMBER   The Damned's manager Jake Riviera undermines the solidarity of the tour by suggesting that all the groups play without the Pistols (since the bans only apply to them). Malcolm, rightly, ejects the Damned from the tour.

13 DECEMBER   Except for Siouxsie and Severin, who are rehearsing in Denmark Street, most of the Pistols' entourage turn up from time to time at various stages of the tour.

STRUMMER AND ROTTEN

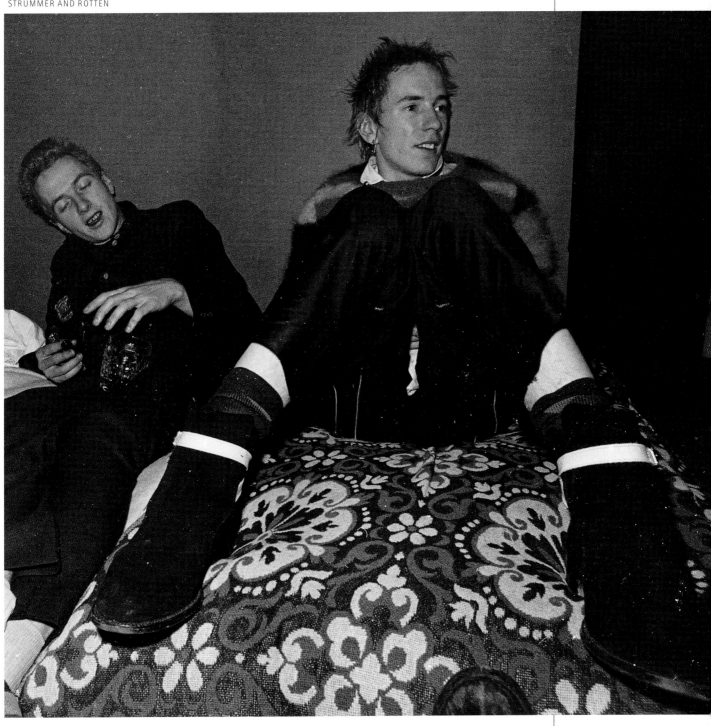

There's fuck all to do but sit in hotel bars and bedrooms, get pissed
and hide from reporters who are dogging us everywhere, and I'm running
out of speed. But it's nice sleeping in proper beds for a change.

14 DECEMBER

I haven't read Nils's text yet, but I'm sure I'll disagree with most of it. Such is the nature of brothers, and such is the nature of Art. If in fact fashion and music are Arts.

More to the point... At the time of shooting my punk photos (and my hippy photos) I was above all having a good time.
I liked the people and the music. The politics were at best naive.
I enjoyed contributing to the scene, and I enjoyed a second adolescence.

Now I'm an old geezer sitting on a tropical beach in December with fond and hazy memories of an exciting period twenty years ago. Twenty years!

RAY STEVENSON, 1996

22 DECEMBER   End of tour. Broke and cold. To make matters worse, Malcolm hits the roof when he finds out Siouxsie has been using the studio.

25 DECEMBER   Spend X Mass at Caroline Coon's with the chaps. Rotten's made Sid a lovely doll.

HEARTBREAKERS SOUNDMAN KEITH PAUL, JO FAUL, THUNDERS, RAY STEVENSON, NILS, WALTER LURE, PAUL COOK

HEARTBREAKERS BILLY RATH, JERRY NOLAN AND WALTER LURE OUTSIDE 6 DENMARK STREET, 22 DECEMBER

AUNTIE SUE DOLL BY JOHNNY ROTTEN

5 JANUARY

Malcolm was right. EMI have terminated the contract.

6 JANUARY

Siouxsie et al come to the airport to meet the Pistols on their return from Amsterdam. The carefully orchestrated photo opportunity of 'loyal fans greeting group' is a washout, as Ray is the only photographer who bothers to turn up. But the 'fans' help me truck drums, amps and guitars back on the bus, since Malcolm is too tight to hire a van. Malcolm disappears in Vivienne's Mini, the group in cabs. Cunts.

7 JANUARY

Rotten and I are stopped while walking through Soho. The police find some amphetamines on Rots, and he's bundled into a van and taken to West End Central.

17 JANUARY

I'm fed up with it all. Malcolm and Vivienne have become tyrants. If you deviate from or challenge their notions, you're ostracised. Rotten and his mate Wobble, staying in Denmark Street while Steve is off with Nora, are acting like arseholes. I'll take the £300 Malcolm offered and split.

VIVIENNE, MALCOLM, SIOUXSIE, SEVERIN, JONES AND COOK, HEATHROW, 6 JANUARY

SIMONE, SIOUXSIE, SEVERIN, JONES, NILS, DEBBIE, SOPHIE RICHMOND, OLD BILL, HEATHROW, 6 JANUARY

Malcolm's fired Glen from the Sex Pistols.

22 JANUARY

Move in with the Heartbreakers whose manager, Leee Black Childers, has got them a deal with Track records. All the Heartbreakers wear ties because they make wonderful tourniquets. Thunders gives me my first shot of heroin, and my paranoid, nervous, amphetamine-fuelled energy is rapidly over-ridden by a wonderful, warm, smacked-out stupor. Thunders wants to get rid of Billy Rath and me to play bass instead. Do some rehearsals in Denmark Street, but I am far too out of it, and playing bass is very boring. I think I'll stick with managing the Banshees.

23 JANUARY

Track give me a retainer to keep them informed about unsigned groups on the punk scene, and pay for the flat I'm sharing with the Heartbreakers and rehearsals for Siouxsie and the Banshees. I shan't sign them to Track, however, because Kit Lambert, the co-owner of Track with Chris Stamp (Terence Stamp's brother), is completely out of his head.

25 JANUARY

WELSH PUNK AT THE ROXY

HEARTBREAKERS JOHNNY THUNDERS AND BILLY RATH

Save Thunders from drowning when he nods out in a plate of spaghetti Bolognese. While we were on the Anarchy Tour, Andrew Czechowski opened the Roxy in Neal Street, Covent Garden. The do-it-yourself ethic is taking off, and, even though the club is pretty unglamorous, it's always busy providing gigs for all the new groups. It's become a regular hang-out since everything closes down so fucking early, including radio and TV which are crap anyway. The politics of boredom.

29 JANUARY

There seem to be zillions of groups and loads of deals going down. I'm still holding off Track.

1 FEBRUARY

Steve and Sid visit the Heartbreakers' Pimlico flat a lot, but they're locked out of the bathroom when me and Thunders get high. We don't want to encourage junkie behaviour, and anyway we haven't got enough dope just to give it away. There are always brilliant girls around.
It's all very rock 'n' roll with the Heartbreakers. Thunders improvises hilarious songs on acoustic guitar, Billy pines for his bird Marcia and Jerry simply craves getting high and eating. Walter reads books.
Paula Yates, a beautiful blonde cleaner, who I met at the Speakeasy, has started staying over.

3 FEBRUARY

Viv Albertine, Mick Jones's girlfriend, has joined up with Sid in the Flowers of Romance. Mail-order companies who advertise in the music papers are selling bondage trousers and vinyl jeans. Even couture designers like Zandra Rhodes are making precious objets d'art out of our worthless totems – jewelled safety pins and the like.

VIV ALBERTINE AND ALAN DRAKE AT THE ROXY

11/28/97

It was the best of times, it was the worst of times, only none of us could tell the difference because we were so out of it all the time. We did everything we weren't supposed to and did it with a vengeance.

What now looks like little more than a "Tempest in a Teapot," at the time it seemed like something really new and different.

London welcomed us with open arms and we had everything we wanted. I even fell in love for about 3 months probably a record.

In any case, like anything new, it soon lost its novelty and the world moved on to some other fad.

Kids screaming for revolution really meant "look a me and gimme more money."

In its end though, we all did cause a little stir + had a fantastic time doing it. And in spite of all the overdoses + burnouts, I really wouldn't have changed a thing.

Walter Lure

WALTER LURE, 1997

WALTER LURE

T.V. SMITH AND GAYE ADVERT INTERVIEW EACH OTHER

The Roxy wasn't like any other club we'd been to, was it? What was different?

It had a unique atmosphere – the focal point of what was going on. You didn't just go when there was a band you wanted to see, you just went there. Looking back, we were really lucky to do our first gigs there instead of in some church hall or something.

Let's describe the place. There was usually a small queue into Neal St., then you'd get past Andy, who'd do the door himself usually, and you'd be in the upstairs bar, tiny, like a little corridor . . . . and get a beer off Des the barman . . . Don Letts' brother, wasn't he? Everyone would pack in shoulder to shoulder in this little space, holding their cans of beer. There was a room with tables and chairs off to one side, but no-one went in there . . . except Tony Parsons and Julie Burchill. There were always interesting people to talk to – Wayne County (as was) gave me a pair of shades once when we supported him early on. You felt you were with friends. You'd hang around talking to people you'd never met before. Then when a band started playing the upstairs bar would clear. You'd go down that narrow flight of stairs to the basement. You could see the stage from the side as you went down.

After the club had been open a couple of weeks and word was getting round, the room would be packed. The first time we played it was only half-full. People stood back and I went off the stage with the microphone and sang right in front of them. It seemed pretty daring. Afterwards, Rotten told me "you shouldn't do that – your place is on the stage."

How did you feel about playing at the Roxy?

I wasn't made to feel conscious of the fact that I was female there as I was by the music press – a band full of Marians could have played there and no one would have batted an eyelid!

I could sing the lyrics I wanted to and we could put across the style and feel of the band the way we wanted. No-one directed us. We couldn't have got away with it anywhere else.

T.V. Smith   Gaye

T.V. SMITH AND GAYE ADVERT, 1998

THE ADVERTS, AT THE ROXY

GAYE ADVERT

THE FIRST ARTICLE TO APPEAR IN THE BRITISH MUSIC PRESS ON EATER WAS BY JONH INGHAM OF SOUNDS, AUTUMN 1976. IT WAS AN A-Z ROUND UP OF ALL THE PUNK ROCK BANDS SO FAR — THERE WEREN'T THAT MANY OF US AT THE TIME — JUST THE PISTOLS, THE CLASH, DAMNED AND THE BUZZCOCKS.

FOR THE NEXT THREE YEARS, WE FOUND OURSELVES TO BE VERY BUSY. OF COURSE THE CHANGE OF LIFESTYLE WAS WELCOME. ONE MINUTE WE WERE AWKWARD, SLIGHTLY NERDY ADOLESCENTS, THE NEXT WE WERE HOMETOWN HEROES WITH A SURFEIT OF 'IN DEPTH' SOCIOLOGICAL JOURNALISTIC FEATURES ON US. OUR AGES (14-16) MEANT THAT WE WERE NEVER TAKEN THAT SERIOUSLY, BUT FOR A BUNCH OF LADS THAT, UP UNTIL NOW, HAD RARELY EVER BEEN OUT TO GIGS OURSELVES, IT WAS QUITE A FEAT.

THERE WERE QUITE A FEW CHANGES IN OUR YOUNG LIVES THAT WE HAD TO ADAPT TO — E.G: ONE NIGHT WE'D BE BEING DRIVEN AROUND LONDON WITH THE CLASH, GATECRASHING POSH MUSIC BIZ PARTIES, MEETING OUR POP STAR HEROES WHILST DISCUSSING PUNK'S RELEVANCE, TAKING SPEED AND 'GETTING OFF' WITH GIRLS, MANY (AND IN SOME CASES — MANY, MANY) YEARS OLDER THAN OURSELVES. THE NEXT MORNING WE'D BE BACK AT SCHOOL, THROWING PAPER AEROPLANES AT TEACHER. IT WAS A BRILLIANT DOUBLE LIFE!

ALTHOUGH A LOT OF CRITICISM WAS THROWN AT THE PUNK SCENE'S "CLIQUEY-NESS", FOR MYSELF (AND, I RECKON, MOST OF THE OTHERS INVOLVED IN THE ORIGINAL 'FIRST WAVE BANDS) — IT WAS THIS SEPERATISM THAT MADE IT ALL SO SPECIAL. TAKING THE PISS OUT OF THE PROVINCIAL NEW-COMERS WAS ALL PART OF THE FUN. PUNK ROCK UNNOFFICIALLY DIED ON THE DAY THE NATIONAL PRESS GOT HOLD OF IT. SHAME THAT.

— ANDY BLADE —
— (EATER) —
— NOV. 1997. —

ANDY BLADE, 1997

DEE GENERATE AND ANDY BLADE OF EATER ON THE STAIRS OF THE ROXY

EATER AT THE ROXY

DEE GENERATE AND SALLY

Eater are the youngest group around. They're still at school.
Dee Generate, their drummer, is only fourteen, and a lot of people
want to fuck him. Leee Black Childers has taken Eater under
his wing.

7 FEBRUARY

INTERIOR, THE ROXY

23 FEBRUARY	It's finally happened – Sid's joined the Sex Pistols.
24 FEBRUARY	The Banshees play their first gig at the Red Deer, Croydon, supporting the Heartbreakers. The group's line-up is Siouxsie, naturally, Peter Fenton on guitar, Kenny Morris drums and Steve Severin bass.
8 MARCH	I'm becoming very familiar with the Roxy's toilets, since I spend a lot of time in them, either shagging young punkettes or shooting up whatever I can get my hands on – usually speed, but when the Banshees play I can afford smack.
10 MARCH	Wayne County's been playing in New York since the early days of Glam. He and other New Yorkers, who failed to get their fifteen minutes in the States, are trucking over to England to try their luck. Like Wayne County, Cherry Vanilla failed to make it as part of Bowie's American entourage. She's turned up here playing with session musicians like Sting, Andy Summers and Stewart Copeland.
16 MARCH	Pistols thrown off A&M after less than a week.

WAYNE COUNTY, AT DINGWALLS

CHERRY VANILLA AND STING, AT DINGWALLS, 15 MARCH

Punk to me was one long party. Sex was fashionable & bi-sexuality was in (there were lots of cute guys & girls). Parents were freaking out about their offspring & politicians & heads of state were up in arms about the decline in Moral Standards, even the Queen was wearing a safety Pin thru her nose.

I remember my 21st birthday. A girlfriend & I stole a car & trekked across Town to the Hope & Anchor — The Punk Pub — where the Jam were playing. Then we went to Dingwalls In camden to see Cherry Vanilla, The aging Andy warhol starlett. In the Early hours of the Morning I found Myself at the Speakeasy, The best club of all. Anyone who was anyone went there. That night the Heart breakers were playing.

After the gig I went back to the heart breakers flat In Pimlico with Nils, who also lived there. Nancy Spungen was in the living room doning on about Meeting the Sex Pistols, she obviously had her heart set on getting one — Anyone! She had arrived from N.Y. that afternoon & the band wouldent let her in. But Nils told her she could (Much to everyones horror). Later that night
stay) ← Johny Thunders locked himself in his bedroom & Jerry Nolan got into bed with Me & Nils, fully clothed. He was scared stiff of being alone with Nancy on the Loose.
Johny & Jerrys Paranoia later proved Justified

Simone xoxo

SIMONE

NANCY SPUNGEN AT THE ROXY

20 MARCH   Thunders and Jerry force Nancy to move from the flat to Linda's. I don't understand what all the fuss is about - she's just a junkie groupie.

SEX PISTOLS FANS AT NOTRE DAME HALL, 28 MARCH

YOUNG FAN AT NOTRE DAME HALL, 28 MARCH

DAVE VANIAN OF THE DAMNED AT NOTRE DAME HALL, 28 MARCH

28 MARCH

Sid's bass-playing is worse than mine. He'll be the spanner in the works. It's all rather gone to his head and he's become a terrible bully. He recently whacked me over the head with a bottle when I tried to stop him hitting little Debbie at a party. It didn't smash, and luckily I was so out of it, I barely felt a thing. Sid was so shocked that I didn't collapse, he legged it. Another time Sid attacked me with a chain. I called him out and he backed down.

29 MARCH

The nihilism of the Pistols is countered by the positivism of the Clash going on about collective action and radical left-wing politics. They are a lot easier to understand than the Pistols, and since they signed their £100,000 deal with CBS they've become the blueprint for the 'punk' group. It's difficult to like both bands, but Vivienne reckoning they've got it all wrong implies there is something to get right. I doubt that Viv is even aware of all the chancers coming up, like Sham 69.

SID VICIOUS ON STAGE WITH THE PISTOLS, 28 MARCH

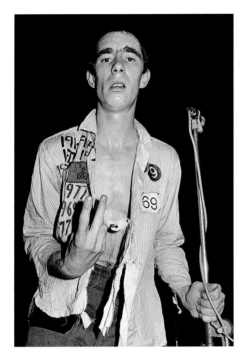

JIMMY PURSEY OF SHAM 69

THE CLASH

THE SLITS, VIV KNEELING

We didn't have to pretend to be nice girls. We didn't have to dress, talk, act or write about being nice girls. It was a liberation. And we weren't the freaks, everyone else was.

Viv

VIV ALBERTINE, 1997

DON LETTS AND ARI UP, MUSIC MACHINE

1977 EVERY GENERATION NEEDS ITS
OWN SOUNDTRACK. I HAD MINE
'DREADLOCKS DREAD'. THE CLASH,
THE SLITS AND THE PISTOLS WERE
MAKING THIERS-REBEL MUSIC. I
WAS THE D.J AT THE ROXY, BACK
IN THE DAY WHEN YOU HAD ONE
DECK AND TWO SPLIFFS!
THE PUNKS PICKED UP GUITARS-I
PICKED UP A SUPER-8. SHOOTING
FROM THE HIP CAME THE PUNK ROCK
MOVIE. I·TECH OUTTAKES:
THE NIGHT STRUMMER CAME TO THE
HOUSE OF DREAD 'WHITEMAN IN
HAMMERSMITH PALAIS'. JEANNETTE
WATCHING KNOWINGLY FROM THE WINGS
AS PATTI SMITH HANDED ME HER MIKE,
AND TAPPER ZUKIE HER GUITAR IN
FRONT OF 5000. YOU SEE JEANNETTE
KNEW DON CAN'T SING AND THE ZUKIE
CAN'T PLAY: 'LIGHTNING FLASH AND THE
WEAKHEART DROP'. EXPLAINING TO BOB
THAT THE PUNKS WERE'NT CRAZY
BALDHEADS, THEY WERE MY FRIENDS,
AND YES MY BONDAGE TROUSERS WERE
COOL. MALICE IN GANJALAND-ROTTEN
TAKING ME TO JAMAICA FOR THE
FIRST TIME: PRINCE FARI - BIG YOUTH·
U·ROY 'PUNKY REGGAE PARTY'.

DON LETTS, 1997

DON LETTS AND ARI UP

Nora's daughter, the fourteen-year-old singer of the Slits, Ari Up, is
a live one. Last night at the Roxy she attacked Paul Cook with a knife.
It left a huge hole in the back of the leather jacket he stole from
Malcolm. But I love the racket the Slits make – their gigs are as
unpredictable as Ari's mood swings. Between playing brilliant dub sounds
and working at Boy in King's Road, Don Letts is filming everything.

1 APRIL

THE SLITS, WOOLWICH

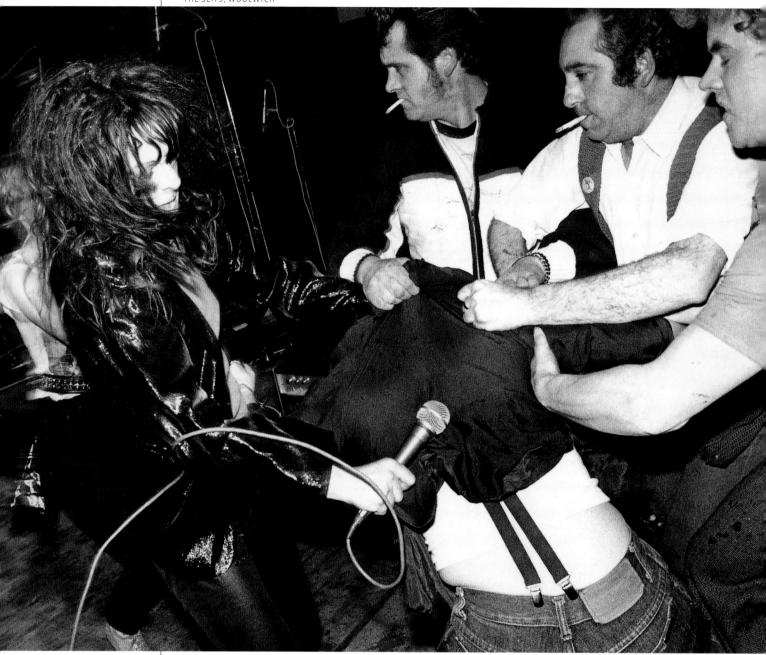

10 MAY

Viv and Malc are obsessed with '50s rock 'n' roll and jive well together, so it was no surprise when Viv had a go at me when I bought Patti Smith's first album 'Horses'. I explained that it was the best record around, but she insists that the best around isn't good enough. 'Be reasonable, demand the impossible,' as the Situationists used to say. I still quite like Patti Smith though.

PATTI SMITH

BOOGIE WITH BILLY IDOL OUTSIDE CRACKERS AKA THE VORTEX, 4 JUNE

4 JUNE   While we're away on the Heartbreakers' tour, the Vortex opens in Soho. John Tiberi aka Boogie is now Pistols' tour-manager.

The first time i heard Anarchy in the UK, Jayne County (then wayne) was playing it at Max's Kansas City. I ran over & said - WHO's THIS?!? it was the most exciting record i'd heard in ages. I arrived in london soon after & went straight from the plane to the Heartbreakers gig at Dingwall's & when they played the Roxy. I remember saying to Leee Black Childers - but the boys don't look cute looking like THAT!, & Leee said - you'll get used to it. I DID & STAYED - i went on tour with the Heartbreakers & for 2 years i was living my fantasy - SEX, & DRUGS, & Rock n' ROLL the dream was the sex & the rock n' roll - the nightmare was the drugs. and since i didn't take drugs - there was plenty of drinks!

GAIL HIGGINS, 1997

Gail higgins
aka hooperys lens
aka Sparkle Moore

GAIL HIGGINS ON HEARTBREAKERS' TOUR COACH

MAGENTA DE VINE

Hook up with an amazing Amazon at Boomtown Rats gig in Hertfordshire. She's called Magenta - very posh. End up back at her parents' house, swimming pool, horses, and, most important, a well-stocked bar. I crash in her parents' room, but am surprised by the naked Magenta stealing across the room to the bed I'm trying to sleep in. She's lovely! My notoriety within this small clique more than compensates for having no money. You couldn't buy this life.

6 JUNE

The Vortex, which opened with the Buzzcocks, the Fall and John Cooper Clarke, holds a lot more people than the Roxy. With a legal capacity of 600, you can cram in many more punters than that. It becomes our staple source of income. Style commentators like Peter York are hovering. Steve Harington, aka Steve Strange, has moved to London. He used to be an obsessive Pistols' fan. I would drop him off in the middle of nowhere after Pistols' gigs in Wales. A peculiar sight disappearing over the hills in the dead of night in full Welsh punk (the most outrageous) regalia.

7 JUNE

Virgin arrange an 'alternative' celebration for the Queen's Jubilee with a boat trip down the River Thames. Neither Ray nor I are invited, thank God, since the boat is boarded by the police and a lot of people are arrested. Paul Cook tells me Malcolm and Vivienne are thrilled by the experience of being incarcerated, whereas for him and Steve Jones it wouldn't have been an exactly novel experience.

8 JUNE

The psychos are taking over and the camp element are abandoning ship. Alan Jones, who was one of the most interesting dressers, is one of the first to drift away. It really isn't his scene any more.

GENE OCTOBER OF CHELSEA AND PETER YORK AT THE VORTEX

STEVE STRANGE AT THE VORTEX

I loved wearing the clothes, although I'd always get aggro in the street, and arrested that infamous time. I loved the music, the Nashville & the EL Paradise gigs I remember like they were yesterday. I loved going to Louise's club in Poland Street & talking to the boys (the Pistols) upstairs in the bar all night, and then shagging the boys downstairs in the toilets! What I never bought though were the politics. I didn't care about any of that and — if they were honest — no one else did really either. Once Punk became less of a fun fashion thing and more violent — the Jubilee Boat Party was the turning point for me — I gave up, started wearing Village People leather outfits and moved on to Roller Disco!

Alan Jones

ALAN JONES, 1997

ALAN JONES, WITH JORDAN AND LINDA

SIOUXSIE AND THE BANSHEES

20 JULY

Since John McKay replaced Peter Fenton, the Banshees have really gelled and have been playing all over the country. They are rapidly becoming one of the biggest draws on the scene even though they haven't got a record deal or any equipment except for two guitars. I have to borrow amps and drums or make sure they have support groups who have drum kits and amps. It's ridiculous.

16 AUGUST

A red-letter day. Danny Baker strides on the Vortex stage and announces that Elvis is dead. The audience cheer. Baker panics and starts claiming that we wouldn't be here if it weren't for the King. A barrage of glasses are hurled at him and he dashes from the stage. He is very upset.

20 OCTOBER

You don't need to contrive stunts to antagonise the authorities. Siouxsie, Banshees drummer Kenny Morris and Pablo la Britain of 999 are arrested while waiting for a cab after supporting the Heartbreakers at the Rainbow, charged with obstruction, thrown in jail and fined the following morning. Siouxsie's brief implies that the police sergeant who testified against Siouxsie and Kenny has it in for us, and that we should keep well away from Finsbury Park. The fascist regime.

25 OCTOBER

Since the Buzzcocks supported the Pistols in Manchester last year, they've developed a great pop sensibility with terrific songs like 'Orgasm Addict', and Pete Shelley's so suburban-camp.

28 OCTOBER

Billy Idol, who was to be guitarist in the Banshees, has now left Chelsea and formed Generation X.

PETE SHELLEY OF THE BUZZCOCKS, WOOLWICH

GENERATION X, MARQUEE DRESSING ROOM

SIOUXSIE AND JORDAN AT ERIC'S CLUB, LIVERPOOL

JORDAN AND ADAM AND THE ANTS, MARQUEE, 12 NOVEMBER

ADAM ANT AND SIOUXSIE

RICHARD HELL OF RICHARD HELL AND THE VOIDOIDS, MUSIC MACHINE, 14 NOVEMBER

Adam and his Ants are still singing about lust and perversion with songs like 'Whip In My Valise' and 'Deutsche Girls', so they have become a regular support act for us. Adam's a handsome boy and he soaks up ideas like a sponge. Jordan is managing them, which is convenient. She has taken to applying a Mondrian to her face. Beautiful. She takes to the stage for one song about Andy Warhol. A stage is too small for her.

12 NOVEMBER

Siouxsie co-headlines the Music Machine with Richard Hell of the original spiky haircut and distressed clothing. Some little bastard in the audience headbuts me and runs away. He can't be more than fifteen. It fucking hurts though. Spend much of the evening trying to find him, but to no avail. I don't know how Siouxsie copes with playing to these arseholes, screaming to see her tits, grabbing her legs and gobbing at her. I get immense pleasure when she raps one of the wankers with a mike stand or kicks someone on the head who's too amorous, though they probably like it.

14 NOVEMBER

THE STRANGLERS

15 NOVEMBER

Accepting the call of the stage means being subjected to the rage of the audience. Performers have become like medieval witches, the stage the stocks where they are held captive, recipients of spit, projectiles and abuse. The Stranglers have the most obnoxious fans called the Finchley Boys.

SID, NANCY AND KIDS, IVANHOE'S, HUDDERSFIELD, X MASS 1977

23 DECEMBER

Gatecrash the Polydor records party at the Valbonne where Siouxsie worked as a waitress until the Grundy incident, after which momentous entertainment she was sacked. Get completely pissed and badger A&R men Alan Black and Chris Parry into a meeting with me re the Banshees.

25 DECEMBER

Ray's bravely gone to see the Pistols who are playing at a benefit for the children of firemen and one-parent families in Huddersfield.

27 DECEMBER

Mark P has been producing a fanzine called 'Sniffin Glue' for some time, he's got a group, too, called Alternative TV. I don't think he likes us.

X-Ray Spex aren't just another stereotypical punk group. Good songs full of irony, about fakery and commodified culture.

POLY STYRENE OF X-RAY SPEX, ROUNDHOUSE

MARK P

FOR ME, PUNK MEANT AN ESCAPE FROM A VERY BORING JOB IN BANKING. IT GAVE ME THE CHANCE TO BE CREATIVE AND SHARE MY IDEAS WITH OTHERS WHO SEEMED TO BE ON THE SAME WAVELENGTH AS ME.

IN EARLY 1977 I FELT THAT I COULD CHANGE THE WORLD - WE WERE IN ACTION, WE HAD THE TIME, WE HAD THE VISION.

IT WASN'T JUST PUNK "ROCK". SNIFFIN GLUE, SEX PISTOLS, THE CLASH ... IT WAS ART IN ACTION....

UNTIL THE BIG RECORD COMPANIES MOVED IN AND PACKAGED THE WHOLE THING - BY THE END OF '77 PUNK WAS DEAD. I MOVED ON OUT PUNK STUCK TO US LIKE A INCURABLE DISEASE. I SUFFERED FROM PUNK AND STILL DO.

THAT FIRST YEAR, JULY '76 TO JULY '77 WAS THE REAL DEAL.

MARK PERRY.

MARK PERRY, 1998

CHARLIE HARPER OF UK SUBS

14 JANUARY Pistols split up in the USA after their Winterland gig.

15 JANUARY The whole punk thing is snowballing. Malcolm's phrase 'dole-queue rock' now seems appropriate as bands all over have started demanding inclusion, with songs like Chelsea's 'the right to work' (the last thing I want to do), and about collective action as in Sham 69's, 'If the kids are united, we will never be divided.' In fact, all new groups are tarred with the same punk brush, though Malcolm's preferred phrase New Wave is starting to be applied to benign groups like the Police and Elvis Costello. I'm not interested in any of that. I just need a hit. But since the Heartbreakers have gone back to New York, I determine to get straight, and suffer dreadful cold turkey.

16 JANUARY Go back to Mum's house in Finchley. It's freezing in the house. I feel like shit. This is hell.

STIV BATORS OF THE DEAD BOYS

STRUMMER, SIMONON AND JONES, ROCK AGAINST RACISM, 30 MARCH

GROWING UP IN LONDON THERE WAS ALWAYS THE FEAR THAT YOU COULD RUN INTO ONE OF THE MANY GANGS THAT STALKED THE CITY STREETS, BE IT THE TEDDY BOYS, ~~THE~~ SKINHEADS OR THE FOOTBALL MOB!

1977 ~~HERALDED~~ THE ARRIVAL OF 'PUNK' MANY OF THE GANGS FELT THREATENED BY THIS NEW GROUP AND PUT ASIDE THEIR DIFFERENCES AND TURNED ON IT.

AFTER MUCH THUMPING AND BASHING THE 'PUNK WARS' FINALLY CAME TO AN END!

BLAH BLAH AND WE WON
BLAH BLAH BLAH.

PAUL SIMONON, 1997   P. SIMONON

TOYAH WILCOX

Rock against Racism Concert, Finsbury Park. Everyone's taking a stand against the common enemy, the National Front. The NF are becoming powerful, so there's no longer any irony or glamour in the stockings and swastikas that signified the decadence of pre-war Berlin and pissed off your parents.

STEEL PULSE

SHANE MCGOWAN, OF THE NIPPLE ERECTORS, MUSIC MACHINE, 21 MAY

21 MAY — Shane, the one-time Pistols and Clash fan who went to Westminster school, has formed a group called the Nipple Erectors.

25 MAY — It's all getting a bit serious and right on. People like Alan Jones revelled in being perverts, and outsiders (the Other), and drew attention to themselves with outrageous slogans and clothes. Now there's a new liberal politic that craves tolerance and understanding: inclusion rather than exclusion. But without 'the Other' there's nowhere to go. Spend the night doing freebase in Hammersmith.

9 JUNE — Finally sign the Banshees to Polydor.

1 JULY — Recording at Olympic Studios. After three days, realise that it's the drummer not the room that produces the Led Zep sound, knock it on the head, and enrol Steve Lillywhite to co-produce Siouxsie and the Banshees' first single 'Hong Kong Garden'. Must buy Kenny a drum kit.

23 JULY — Patch it up with John Curd who's promoting the Banshees at the Roundhouse.

ROADENT AND SOUNDS JOURNALIST JANE SUCK

As a provincial plebian from the provinces, it was ~~bloody~~ ~~thing~~ exciting to be part of something where it seemed that the sum of the parts was more than the whole.

There was a sense that those of us on the periphery were as important as those at the centre.

Of course I was deluded.

But during the delusion I felt that we were the one eyed men in the valley of the blind.

Of The times I haven't much to say, except that since, we have all been trailing an Albatross wake of expectation.

Roadent

ROADENT, 1998

Roadent, one-time Clash and now Pistols roadie, won a scholarship and attended some public school or other. Like Rotten, he stubs cigarettes out on his arms. He's very bright.

4 SEPTEMBER

Move to Chelsea Cloisters. Now I've got fucking hepatitis.

5 SEPTEMBER

'Hong Kong Garden' Number 7 in the charts and Siouxsie has split up with Severin. Yes! Seize my chance and move in on her. Don't want anyone to know, as it could cause friction and jealousy within the group.

13 SEPTEMBER

20 SEPTEMBER

Fachtna O'Ceallaigh, the Boomtown Rats manager, invites us to a big party at Putney swimming baths. Everyone's waiting for the man with the coke. When he finally arrives, someone stupidly throws him in the pool. Typical.

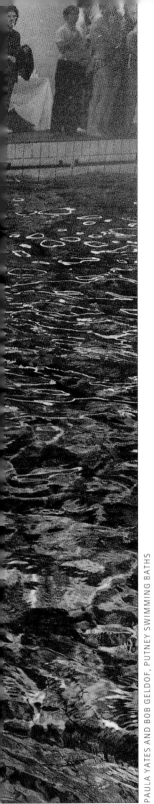

PAULA YATES AND BOB GELDOF, PUTNEY SWIMMING BATHS

BILLY IDOL

ULTRAVOX

CHRISSIE HYNDE

JOHN CURD, PROMOTER

Sitting in a West london flat with a member of a 'revolutionary' (it was easy in those days, all you needed were the right clothes and the right price) punk group and him saying: "Don't let anyone know I've been here, Bernie wouldn't like it."

'Police and Thieves' by Junior Murvin, 'Bodies' by the Pistols and 'Born For A Purpose' by Dr. Alimantado.

Being riddled with guilt at being an Irishman in london while just a couple of hundred miles away in my own country, the Brits and their willing lackeys were busily murdering, torturing, looting and pillaging their way through the streets of West Belfast and around the botharins of South Armagh and other rural areas.

Fachtna ó Ceallaigh
Dec. 1997.

FACHTNA O'CEALLAIGH

FACHTNA O'CEALLAIGH, 1997

12 OCTOBER Sid's gone all the way. He's been charged with murdering Nancy at the Chelsea Hotel. I feel creepy.

28 OCTOBER Rent a fuck-off Merc limo for the 'Scream' UK tour. It's brilliant to speed past all the other tossers in their street-cred transits and lumbering tour buses. My secret meetings with Siouxsie are adding a perverse excitement to our affair.

Sid o.d.s in New York. Poor Sid. He believed the myth.

Polydor decide to come down on bootlegggers, using us for a trial run at some small hustler, not that I ever gave a toss about other people making a few bob out of the Banshees. But a mate of the bootlegger takes offence and, after plying me and Siouxsie with champagne at the Oxford street club he runs, he gets a bunch of his cronies to give me a beating. Now we need bodyguards. From now on people are going to pay.

Every screwball and chancer is forming a band or record label. Even the Pistols have become just another commodity, and buying the product, rather than creating it, negates its meaning. Malcolm and Jamie use this paradox to promote the 'Great Rock 'n' Roll Swindle' soundtrack.

ONE OF THE MOD-ETTES LOST IN THE SUPERMARKET, JANUARY

RICHARD JOBSON OF THE SKIDS

NEW MOD, BRIGHTON

PAUL WELLER OF THE JAM

LYNVAL GOULDING AND JERRY DAMMERS OF THE SPECIALS

SECRET AFFAIR

BILLY IDOL ON STAGE WITH LEVI AND THE ROCKCATS

Actions rarely have the desired effect. All the discontent and left-wing politics has united the extreme right and centre. The election is won by the Conservatives and Margaret Thatcher is Prime Minister.

Musically, everything is permitted now. Ska through Two Tone with the Specials and Selecter; mod revival in Secret Affair and the Jam; rockabilly with Levi and the Rockcats; and reggae with Steel Pulse, Reggae Regular and Lynton Kwesi Johnson getting critical acclaim. Significantly, none of these factions are fighting with each other.

THE JAM, LONDON PALLADIUM

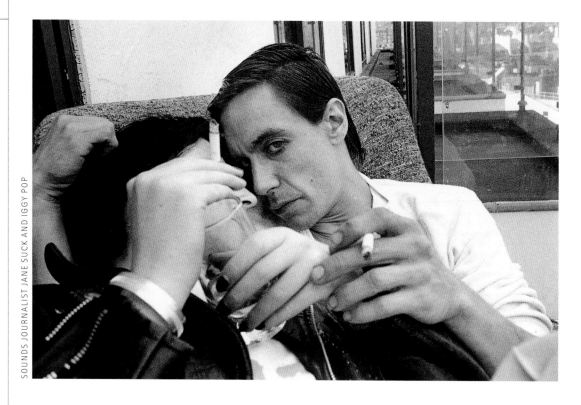

SOUNDS JOURNALIST JANE SUCK AND IGGY POP

7 MAY

Producing Banshees' second album 'Join Hands' with Marc Bolan's former engineer Mike Stavrou. McKay and Morris are behaving like dickheads.

22 MAY

Visit Rotten, who's living with Nora! Neither of us mentions Sid.

7 SEPTEMBER

In Aberdeen, Morris and McKay split before the second date of our first major national tour – all our money is tied up in it. Ask Cook, who I'm living with, and Jones to join the Banshees. Jonesy is up for it, but Cook isn't. Robert Smith from our support group the Cure agrees to play one set with the Cure, then one with the Banshees. Cancel four gigs, persuade Budgie to leave the Slits, and the tour is off again.

9 OCTOBER

If it weren't for his huge alcohol intake, Robert Smith would be a perfect replacement for McKay, but he won't leave the Cure.

10 OCTOBER

Go out for dinner with Iggy, who tries to impress Siouxsie by singing and dancing in the street, and shovelling up food with his hands.

15 DECEMBER

Brian Setzer, ex-Bloodless Pharaohs, is over from New York, playing with his new group the Stray Cats. He's great, but he won't leave them.

PAULINE BLACK, SELECTER, ELECTRIC BALLROOM, 21 JULY

SIOUXSIE WITH ROBERT SMITH OF THE CURE, 9 OCTOBER

STRAY CATS, BRIAN SETZER LEFT

20 DECEMBER

Blondie are like a '60s pop band, and yet even they are hailed as a punk band. What does it all mean? Nevertheless, go to the Blondie X Mass party at Notre Dame Hall and bump into Kenny Morris there. Naturally it all ends in tears. Siouxsie throws the first punch and then I steam in.

SIOUXSIE, NILS, STEVE SEVERIN AND KENNY MORRIS PUNCH-UP AT BLONDIE PARTY

124

BOY GEORGE, HELEN, SIOUXSIE, MARILYN AND ZIGZAG JOURNALIST KRIS NEEDS, BLONDIE PARTY

1980

20 FEBRUARY

It isn't fun any more. I've become a responsible manager with a difficult relationship with Siouxsie and a business to run. John has dropped his Rotten moniker, returning to his real name Lydon for his new group Public Image Ltd. Cook and Jones are being managed by John Curd and hanging round with old rock stars like Pete Townshend and Phil Lynott. New Romantics are returning to the origins of punk style with the Bowie nights at Gossips. Adam has enrolled Marco and is becoming a pop pin-up. Malcolm and Vivienne believe they are fashion designers now rather than shopkeepers, and are preparing a catwalk show, having changed the name of the shop to World's End.

27 AUGUST

Holidaying in LA with Siouxsie. Stay at the Chateau Marmont, and rent a bright yellow Merc convertible. Polydor have picked up their option. It seems I have a future after all.

NILS AND SIOUXSIE, SANTA MONICA BEACH, LOS ANGELES, 27 AUGUST 1980

BIBLIOGRAPHY

Albert, J, and Albert, S, (eds), *The Sixties Papers*,
    Praeger 1984

Barbrook, R, *Media Freedom*, Pluto Press,
    London 1995

Benjamin, W, *Illuminations*, Fontana, London 1973

Berlin, I, *Against the Current*, Oxford University
    Press, Oxford 1981

Campbell, C, *The Romantic Ethic And The Spirit
    Of Modern Consumerism*, Basil Blackwell,
    Oxford 1987

Connor, S, *Postmodernist Culture*, Basil Blackwell,
    Oxford 1989

Debord, G, *The Society of the Spectacle*,
    Zone, New York 1994

Femie, E, *Art History and its Methods*,
    Phaidon, London 1995

Fiske, J, *Understanding Popular Culture*,
    Unwin Hymann, Boston 1989

Green, J, *Days In The Life*, Minerva, London 1988

Howes, K, *Broadcasting It*, Cassell, London 1993

Marcus, G, *Lipstick Traces*, Penguin,
    Harmondsworth 1989

Mizejewski, L, *Divine Decadence*,
    Princeton University Press, New Jersey 1992

Plant, S, *The Most Radical Gesture*, Routledge,
    London 1992

Redhead, S, *The End of the Century Party*,
    Manchester University Press, Manchester 1990

Renan, S, *The Underground Film*, Studio Vista,
    London 1967

Savage, J, *England's Dreaming*, Faber and Faber,
    London 1991

Vague, T, *Anarchy In The UK: The Angry Brigade*,
    AK Press, Edinburgh 1997

Vermorel, F, *Fashion and Perversity*, Bloomsbury,
    London 1996

Withers, J, *Impresario: Malcolm McLaren,
    The British New Wave* (exhibition catalogue),
    MIT, Cambridge Mass. 1998

York, P, *Style Wars*, Sidgwick and Jackson,
    London 1980

MEANWHILE GARDENS, WEST LONDON, 1980

INDEX